P9-CQJ-460

0 00 30 0330670 5

Killer
Superbugs

Killer Superbugs

The Story of Drug-Resistant Diseases

Nancy Day

Enslow Publishers, Inc.

40 Industrial Road   PO Box 38
Box 398   Aldershot
Berkeley Heights, NJ 07922   Hants GU12 6BP
USA   UK

http://www.enslow.com

Library of Congress Cataloging-in-Publication Data

Day, Nancy, 1953–
    Killer superbugs : the story of drug-resistant diseases / Nancy Day.
        p. cm. — (Issues in focus)
    Includes bibliographical references and index.
    ISBN 0-7660-1588-2 (hard)
    1. Drug resistance in microorganisms—Juvenile literature.
[1. Drug resistance in microorganisms.] [DNLM: 1. Drug Resistance,
Microbial—Popular Works. 2. Antibiotics—therapeutic use—Popular
Works. 3. Bacteria—drug effects—Popular Works. 4. Bacterial
Infections—drug therapy—Popular Works. 5. Viruses—drug effects—
Popular Works. WB 330 D274k 2001] I. Title. II. Issues in focus
(Hillside, N.J.)
    QR177 .D395   2001
    616'.01—dc21
                           00-012458

Printed in the United States of America

10 9 8 7 6 5 4 3 2 1

To Our Readers: We have done our best to make sure all Internet
addresses in this book were active and appropriate when we went to
press. However, the author and the publisher have no control over and
assume no liability for the material available on those Internet sites or
on other Web sites they may link to. Any comments or suggestions can
be sent by e-mail to comments@enslow.com or to the address on the
back cover.

Illustration Credits: Centers for Disease Control and
Prevention, p. 87; © Corel Corporation, pp. 56, 75, 100; Nancy
Day, pp. 51, 80; Enslow Publishers, Inc., p. 68; National
Library of Medicine, pp. 27, 31, 40, 43, 44, 55, 85; Pfizer,
Inc., pp. 13, 19, 46, 50, 52, 76, 93, 95, 98.

Cover Illustration: © Corbis Stock Market.

Contents

Acknowledgments

Richard A. Falkenrath, Ph.D., assistant professor of public policy, John F. Kennedy School of Government, Harvard University

Pfizer, Inc.

Gregor Reid, Ph.D., M.B.A., professor of microbiology and immunology, The University of Western Ontario, associate scientific director, The Lawson Research Institute

Carl Winter, extension food toxicologist, director, FoodSafe Program, University of California, Davis, California

1

Antibiotic Resistance

Consider the difference in size between some of the very tiniest and the very largest creatures on Earth. A small bacterium weighs as little as 0.00000000001 gram. A blue whale weighs about 100,000,000 grams. Yet a bacterium can kill a whale . . .

—Bernard Dixon, as quoted by Laurie Garrett
in *The Coming Plague: Newly Emerging
Disease in a World Out of Balance*

Two-year-old Dalton Canterbury had been asleep too long. His doctor had said that Dalton just had a case of the flu, but Dalton's mother, Susan Canterbury, was worried. She decided to wake him. That

7

was when she became even more worried. Dalton was so weak he could barely hold up his head. When Dalton's father, Daniel Canterbury, came home from work at 3:00 P.M., he and Susan decided to take Dalton back to the doctor. A test showed that his spinal fluid was cloudy, a sign of bacterial meningitis. Meningitis is an inflammation in the membranes surrounding the brain or spinal cord.

The situation went from bad to worse. Dalton had a seizure in the ambulance on the way to the hospital, another sign that he had meningitis. The doctors decided to fly Dalton from York, Pennsylvania, to Johns Hopkins Hospital in Baltimore, where he could get special care. Susan Canterbury then understood how serious Dalton's condition was. "You mean," she asked, "he could *die*?"[1]

By the time Dalton Canterbury reached Johns Hopkins, he was unconscious and having seizures. The doctors hooked him up to a ventilator, a machine that would breathe for him, and gave him drugs to control the seizures. They did more tests on his spinal fluid and found that a bacterium, *Streptococcus pneumoniae*, was causing the infection.

The next day, the doctors had the full story. Dalton's infection was being caused by a strain of bacteria that would be hard to kill. Tests showed that the bacteria were resistant to (would not be killed by) penicillin, a common antibiotic (drug used to kill bacteria). It was also partially resistant to ceftriaxone, a powerful drug often used to treat meningitis caused by penicillin-resistant bacteria. The doctors' only hope was to give Dalton extremely high doses of ceftriaxone, along with another powerful antibiotic, vancomycin. Vancomycin can kill *Streptococcus pneumoniae*, but it does not get through to the spinal fluid well enough to be used alone.

Three days later, Dalton was still unconscious and having seizures. The most powerful antibiotic weapons medicine could offer were up against a strain of bacteria that had the power to survive antibiotic attacks.[2]

Finally, after two more days of being unconscious, Dalton woke up. He was going to live. It took several weeks for Dalton Canterbury to stand up and longer before he could play normally. As a result of his infection, Dalton's brain was damaged. He may always have seizures and may also have vision and learning problems.[3] But he survived a drug-resistant infection. Thousands of others are not so lucky.

Developing Resistance

Antibiotics are actually nothing new. In fact, they are older than humans—by about 3 billion years. From the earliest days of life on Earth, bacteria and fungi (tiny plants) competed with each other for food and territory. They waged battles to survive. To do this, they used chemical weapons. Then, as now, fungi and bacteria made toxic (poisonous) substances that kill other fungi and bacteria. These substances, called antibiotics, are a natural part of the organisms' defense system.

Unfortunately, these naturally occurring antibiotics were unknown during most of human history.

While these microscopic organisms successfully fought off bacterial enemies, humans died by the millions from infections caused by the same organisms.

While they were using their antibiotic weapons, these ancient bacteria were also evolving, or changing. The changes that helped them survive were passed on. One successful change was developing the ability to resist antibiotic attacks. Bacteria that could resist the antibiotic weapons of other bacteria had a better chance to live and reproduce. The ability to resist antibiotics was then passed on to their offspring. Thus the first antibiotic-resistant bacteria developed well before humans even knew about bacteria, let alone antibiotics.

This natural process is the basis for today's problem with drug-resistant diseases. However, when humans developed and began using antibiotics, they shifted the natural balance. Suddenly, bacteria were facing antibiotics produced by humans as well as those made by other bacteria.

Any time a person takes an antibiotic, it kills some of the hundreds of strains of bacteria in the body. The antibiotic kills the weakest organisms first, whether they are disease-causing bacteria or simply innocent bystanders (harmless or even helpful bacteria). The bacteria that remain may be resistant or partially resistant to the antibiotic. Partially resistant organisms will probably die if the antibiotic treatment continues (the person keeps taking the medication). But if antibiotic treatment stops, partially resistant bacteria may survive. These bacteria are left to reproduce and be spread to other people (or to reinfect the original patient).

Infections caused by resistant bacteria are much harder to stop. The usual treatments take longer to work or do not work at all because the bacteria can fight off the drugs designed to kill them. In some cases, the patient may die before a drug can be found that will kill the bacteria.

Without meaning to, antibiotics "select" resistant bacteria and give them an advantage. This is called selective pressure. Before antibiotics enter the scene, nonresistant bacteria actually have a slight edge because resistant bacteria have to use some of their energy for their antibiotic-fighting skills. But once antibiotics kill off the nonresistant bacteria, the resistant bacteria population can grow. Stuart B. Levy, director of the Center for Adaptation Genetics and Drug Resistance at Tufts University in Boston and author of *The Antibiotic Paradox*, uses the example of weeds growing in a lawn. If the healthy grass is killed off, any surviving weeds (or those that arrive right afterwards) have a wide-open area to spread, free from competition with grass.[4] This means that the use of antibiotics and other chemicals designed to kill bacteria have encouraged resistance by selecting those able to survive antibiotic attack and giving them the opportunity to spread.

Even if the resistant bacteria do not cause disease, they can pass on the ability to resist antibiotics to bacteria that do. Or, harmless but resistant bacteria may now be able to reproduce in such quantities that they become harmful.

The more often an antibiotic is used, the more likely it is that bacteria will develop resistance to it. Common sites for antibiotic-resistant infections include the ear, sinus, throat, lungs, and intestines. People who have weakened immune systems due to age, illness, or medical treatment are more likely to suffer from antibiotic-resistant infections, particularly if they have been in the hospital for a long time.

Organisms that never existed or existed in small numbers in nature are now multiplying into enormous populations, thanks to the advantage of having their competition killed off for them. While these bacteria may be harmless in small numbers, they become dangerous threats when they begin reproducing rapidly inside the human body. And the very skill that has helped them survive—antibiotic resistance—makes them very hard to stop. Levy says that what we are seeing is a massive evolutionary change in bacteria. By developing and using antibiotics, humans have altered the course of history and changed the natural evolution of bacteria.

Penicillin, the most famous antibiotic, was one of the world's greatest medical discoveries. But just four years after drug companies began making it in large quantities, doctors started seeing bacteria that could resist it. These resistant strains were discovered in hospitals, where most of the penicillin was being used. Scientists quickly realized that the resistant hospital strains were different from the slightly resistant strains they had studied in the laboratory. The hospital strains could actually destroy penicillin—

Penicillin mold.

even large amounts of it—so increasing the amount of the miracle drug did not help.

That turned out to be only the first sign of danger. *Staphylococcus* is an organism that is everywhere: in soil, on people's bodies, even on many pets. Normally, the immune system fights it off easily. However, in a person whose immune system is overwhelmed, it can cause a serious infection. Common targets are people with severe burns, premature babies, people with advanced cancer, those who have undergone surgery, and patients in intensive care units. Thanks to penicillin, *Staphylococcus* infections, which were once deadly, had become minor problems. But then *Staphylococcus* started showing signs of resistance.

Researchers developed a new miracle drug: methicillin. This drug worked differently from penicillin and it efficiently killed off *Staphylococcus*. Doctors confidently switched to methicillin during the late 1960s. But by the early 1980s, they started seeing strains that were not only resistant to methicillin but also other, closely related, antibiotics.

Doctors were particularly concerned about methicillin-resistant *Staphylococcus aureus* (MRSA) outbreaks. This organism was found in hospitals, where it attacked people whose immune systems were already being pushed to the limit. Many of them could not survive a massive infection. Scientists studying MRSA were able to trace 470 strains back in time by using the organism's "genetic fingerprint." They discovered that all MRSA bacteria came from a single strain first identified in Cairo, Egypt, in 1961. By the end of the 1960s, strains of MRSA showed up in New York and parts of Canada, Europe, and Africa. Ten years later, MRSA had spread throughout the world. By 1990, MRSA had reached critical levels and hospitals around the world battled it. In 1995, MRSA infections killed 1,409 people in New York City alone.[5]

In 1999, officials at the Centers for Disease Control and Prevention (CDC) reported the first cases in which people who had not become infected in a hospital died from MRSA infections. According to the officials, between 1997 and 1999, MRSA was responsible for at least two hundred illnesses and four deaths in Minnesota and North Dakota. The four deaths were of otherwise healthy children, ages one to thirteen. The children had not been in a hospital or even visited one before their deaths.[6] The bacteria that killed them also seemed to be a slightly different strain from that usually found in hospitals. Researchers were concerned that this was a sign that MRSA was no longer strictly a hospital problem but was now in the general environment.

Doctors are especially concerned about the growing resistance to drugs, such as vancomycin, that are used by doctors as a "last resort" when other antibiotics fail. In the early 1990s, 2 percent of cases involving *Enterococci faecium*, a bacterium that can cause septicemia (a dangerous infection in the bloodstream) in the seriously ill, had become resistant to vancomycin. This strain is called vancomycin-resistant enterococcus faecium, or VREF. VREF spread rapidly and by 1997 vancomycin was unable to control half of all *Enterococcus faecium* bacterial infections.[7]

How Bacteria and Viruses Become Resistant to Drugs

There are several ways that organisms can develop the ability to resist the drugs designed to kill them. One is through natural genetic mutations, or changes, that give some organisms a better ability to resist an attack. For example, bacteria with a mutation that allows them to resist an antibiotic are more likely to survive, while others will be killed by the antibiotic treatment. The survivors reproduce, passing on the successful gene. A single resistant bacterium may produce several billion resistant organisms overnight.

Another way bacteria can pass on a gene for antibiotic resistance is through their sharing of genetic material. The ability to share genetic material helps bacteria survive by providing a way for them to adapt to difficult conditions. One bacterium can pass on the ability to resist a particular drug to another bacterium through this shared genetic material.

Yet another way for bacteria to gain genes for resistance is to pick up plasmids, tiny pieces of DNA that they find in the environment. Bacteria frequently pick up and discard these fragments, which may contain useful skills such as drug resistance. A *Shigella* organism caused a 1968 epidemic in Guatemala that infected 12,500 people. The microbe contained a plasmid that provided resistance to four different antibiotics.[8]

Bacteria trade successful techniques and, in this way, can develop the ability to resist antibiotics before they have even been exposed to them. "Bugs are always figuring out ways to get around the antibiotics we throw at them," said Dr. George Jacoby, of Harvard Medical School. "They adapt, they come roaring back."[9]

Bacteria resist antibiotics in several different ways. One way is for the bacterium to break down the antibiotic. It can do this by making enzymes (substances produced by cells) that attack the antibiotic's chemical structure. Bacteria resistant to penicillins and cephalosporins work this way. Another way is for the bacterium to block the antibiotic from getting inside its cells or to pump it out after it gets in. Resistant strains of *Pseudomonas aeruginosa* function in this way. The last way is for the bacterium to change the target that the antibiotic is designed to seek. The antibiotic is then less able to find and attach itself to the bacterium.

Many bacteria use sporulation, a process that helps them protect themselves against antibiotics or other threats. They toughen up their cell walls and shut down or hibernate while they wait for the threat to pass. Then, when conditions get better, they become active again.

Ever More Resistant Diseases

Increasing populations, poverty, homelessness, and other modern problems promote the spread of infectious disease. This situation is made worse by the increasingly close contact people have with each other. For example, young children often spend time in day care, where they are around children who are sick, often with drug-resistant infections. In one study, the CDC found that a single child at a day-care center in Ohio spread a multi-drug-resistant strain of *Streptococcus pneumoniae* bacteria to other children, staff, and family members. The organism caused drug-resistant ear infections in 20 percent of the children at the day-care center and also spread into the community.[10]

Another reason that the number of antibiotic-resistant infections is rising is the increasing number of people with damaged immune systems. Modern treatments for cancer often reduce the patient's ability to fight off infections. People with acquired immunodeficiency syndrome (AIDS) also have weakened immune systems. When the immune system is not working properly, people must take antibiotics to battle infections that the average person could easily fight off on his or her own.

Doctors treat antibiotic-resistant diseases by trying larger doses of antibiotics, different types of antibiotics, a combination of several antibiotics, or a different means of giving the medication (as a shot instead of a pill, for example). They also use laboratory tests to help them choose the antibiotic that has the best chance of working.

As organisms become resistant to the more commonly known antibiotics, doctors are forced to move on to drugs such as vancomycin. Vancomycin is expensive, must be given by injection, and can cause side effects such as fever, chills, inflammation at the injection site, and damage to the ears and kidneys. But in many cases, it is all that stands between a patient with a raging infection and death. Doctors resort to vancomycin for certain kinds of infections when other antibiotics cannot be used or do not work.

Bacteria and viruses are not the only organisms that can develop resistance. Some parasites (organisms

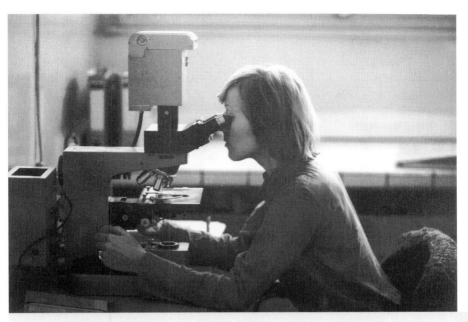

Scientists continue to search for newer, more powerful, and more effective antibiotics.

that live in or on another organism) have the same ability.

Malaria is caused by a parasite that is spread by mosquitoes. It is one of the world's most dangerous infectious diseases. Each year, malaria sickens over 100 million people and kills more than one million.[11] In Africa, malaria kills more people than any other disease except AIDS.[12]

One of the reasons that malaria has become such a killer is that the malaria parasite developed resistance to chloroquine, the only cheap, effective treatment. In some areas, people take chloroquine like aspirin—whenever they have an ache or a pain.

This improper use increases the resistance problem. Now, chloroquine is no longer effective in over eighty of the ninety-two countries where malaria is a major problem.[13] So, the only effective treatment has become almost useless. New drugs are often too expensive for people in developing countries. In addition, the malaria parasite has become resistant to many of these other drugs as well. As a result, the disease is a bigger problem than ever.

Scientists are fascinated by the ability of organisms to develop resistance. The ultimate example is a microbe called *Deinococcus radiodurans*. This organism is the Superman of the bacterial world. It can resist 12 million rads of radiation (a mere one thousand rads kills a human being). It can piece together its own DNA, even after it has been blasted into more than one hundred pieces. It is even able to correct DNA units that have mutated and kick out any that have become damaged. In this way, it keeps itself in perfect condition. Why would bacteria need resistance to levels of radiation so far above any normal level found on Earth? Scientists think that it may be because these skills allow it to live in some less-than-desirable neighborhoods. For example, *Deinococcus radiodurans* has been found in the rock of mountains in Antarctica that have not seen a drop of moisture in thousands of years. It also thrives in deserts. Fortunately, *Deinococcus radiodurans* seems to be content to feed off other bacteria and has no taste for humans.[14]

Major Drug-resistant Organisms and Diseases

As scientists become more concerned about the problem of drug resistance, they are focusing on the diseases that cause the most harm. The major organisms and diseases involved include:

dysentery—An intestinal illness. Up to 90 percent of all cases are resistant to the top two drugs of choice.

gonorrhea—A sexually transmitted disease that increases the risk of infection with HIV and can cause eye infections in infants born to infected women. In some countries, 98 percent of all cases are resistant to penicillin.

human immunodeficiency virus (HIV)—The virus that causes AIDS. It is becoming increasingly resistant to the common treatments.

malaria—A mosquito-borne disease caused by a parasite that has become increasingly resistant to the most popular treatment.

Salmonella—An organism that causes intestinal infections and infections elsewhere in the body. One strain has become resistant to all known antibiotics.

Staphylococcus—A common organism that can turn dangerous. *Staphylococcus aureus* is the leading cause of hospital-acquired infections. Doctors fear this organism will soon become resistant to all antibiotics.

Streptococcus—A common cause of throat and ear infections. It can also cause meningitis, an extremely dangerous infection of the spinal fluid and brain, and pneumonia, a serious lung infection. Up to half of most common forms of meningitis and pneumonia are now resistant to penicillin.

tuberculosis—A highly contagious disease that has become increasingly resistant to treatment.

typhoid—Between 1989 and 1999, eleven countries were hit by epidemics of multi-drug-resistant typhoid fever. Without effective treatment, nearly one in ten people who are infected with *Salmonella typhi* will die.

2

Super Bugs:
Killer Bacteria
and Viruses

The very first requirement in a hospital is that it should do the sick no harm.

—Florence Nightingale

Discovering antibiotics and learning how to manufacture them was certainly one of the most important achievements in human history. However, by developing and using antibiotics to kill disease-causing bacteria and viruses, humans have tampered with the natural world. One result is that these organisms have learned how to resist antibiotics. Some have even learned how to resist many different antibiotics.

23

These multi-drug-resistant organisms, called "super bugs," reproduce and spread to other people, who then develop highly resistant infections.

The Age of the "Super Bug"

Bacteria that can resist one, or even several, antibiotics are a concern. Bacteria that can resist many drugs become a real danger to human populations.

It is these super bugs that worry doctors the most. Doctors are concerned that dangerous bacteria may one day develop resistance to all known antibiotics. This would mean existing treatments would be useless. Infections would be unstoppable and many lives would be lost. A world without effective antibiotics would mean a return to the times when ancient plagues swept through, killing millions, because there were no drugs to stop them.

Super bugs can develop from the use of even a single antibiotic treatment over a long period of time. For example, researchers looked at patients on long-term antibiotic treatment for acne (a skin condition). They found that the acne patients had bacteria that were resistant to three or more antibiotics, even if they had only been treated with one.[1] The important factor was the length of treatment. Long-term antibiotic use promotes resistance to more than one drug.

In a report issued in June 2000, the World Health Organization (WHO) said that diseases that were once easily treated are now often incurable due to the problem of antibiotic resistance. According to the WHO report, "Overcoming Antimicrobial Resistance," illnesses such as tuberculosis, malaria, pneumonia, and even common ear infections have become much more difficult to treat. They blame the problem on misuse of antibiotics, which the report said has reduced the power of "once life-saving medicines to that of a sugar pill."[2]

How big is the threat? Some experts fear that minor disease-causing organisms could become deadly if they develop into super bugs. Others say that the risk of some kind of sweeping plague is low. Mark Goldberger, director of the Food and Drug Administration's division of special pathogen and immunologic drug products, says that most people are not likely to run into a super bug that resists all antibiotics. "For the average person walking around on the street," says Goldberger, "the risk at the moment remains low."[3] Nevertheless, scientists are working hard to develop new drugs for fighting antibiotic-resistant organisms and to try to stay a step ahead of the super bugs.

Hospitals as Breeding Grounds

Each year 2 million people in the United States who spend time in a hospital get something they did not expect—they get sicker.[4] One in twenty of all those admitted to hospitals pick up an infection while there.[5] Although hospitals are where sick people go to get well, they are also, unfortunately, where healthy people can get sick and sick people can become seriously ill or even die.

Sick people coming into hospitals bring a wide

variety of disease-causing bacteria with them. To fight these bacteria, doctors use huge amounts of antibiotics. As a result, hospitals are environments that often produce antibiotic-resistant organisms. Unfortunately, these drug-resistant organisms can then infect people who are in the hospital for other reasons. This happens often enough that these hospital-acquired infections have a special name: nosocomial infections. Of particular concern is that in many cases, the bacteria that cause these infections have survived the rigid infection control practices in hospitals for a very good reason. They are resistant to many different antibiotics.

About 70 percent of the bacteria that cause infections acquired in the hospital are resistant to at least one of the common antibiotics.[6] Drug-resistant diseases can be hazardous enough to an otherwise healthy person. For a hospital patient who is severely ill or whose immune system has been affected by cancer treatments, they can be deadly. Some hospital-acquired infections are resistant to all the approved treatments. In these cases, doctors are forced to use experimental and possibly dangerous drugs to try to stop the infection and save the patient's life.

Hospital-acquired infections are no small problem. Each year they cost $5 billion to treat and kill ninety thousand patients.[7]

Many of the people who are dying of hospital-acquired infections would have survived just five or ten years ago. *Enterococcus*, a usually harmless organism found in the gut, now causes untreatable infections in intensive care units. Some strains of

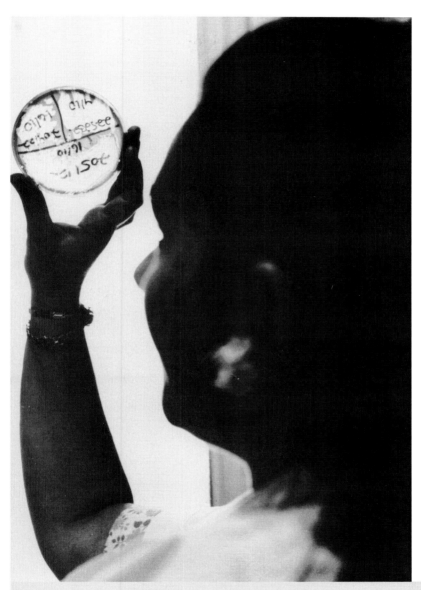

Streptococcus is a common cause of infection. Here, a scientist examines a strep culture growing on an agar plate.

Pseudomonas have become resistant to all known antibiotics. This organism causes potentially fatal respiratory infections in people with cystic fibrosis, a lung disease.

Staphylococcus is the primary cause of hospital-acquired infections. This organism is blamed for 13 percent of the hospital infections each year. Half of the staphylococcal infections contracted by hospital patients in 1997 were resistant to antibiotics (in 1974, only 2 percent were resistant).[8] Although nearly every hospital now has tough infection-control procedures, hospital-acquired infections have become a very serious problem that shows no sign of being solved anytime soon.

Methicillin-resistant *Staphylococcus aureus* (MRSA) infections are becoming more common. The Centers for Disease Control and Prevention (CDC) estimates that eighty thousand people a year get MRSA infections. In the past ten years, the proportion of staphylococcal infections caused by MRSA has gone up to 45 to 50 percent, according to the CDC.[9] While *Staphylococcus aureus* is commonly found on the skin of healthy people and is a common cause of every-thing from pimples to pneumonia, MRSA usually affects people who are already very sick. It can develop in an open wound, be spread by medical devices such as tubes used to drain body fluids, or be passed from person to person. People can also become colonized with MRSA. In these cases, MRSA is on or in the person's body but is not making the person sick. Once doctors discover that a patient is colonized or infected with MRSA, they separate the patient from other patients and tell hospital workers and visitors to use special precautions when in contact with them. This helps prevent the organism from spreading to other people.

Tuberculosis

One hundred years ago people feared tuberculosis as much as people today fear cancer. It was known as "consumption," because it seemed to consume, or eat away, its victims until they died.

Until the 1980s, cases of tuberculosis were declining. Public health officials believed they had it beat. They were wrong. The number of cases surged. By 1993, the World Health Organization had declared tuberculosis a "global emergency." Among the reasons for the trend are increased poverty and malnutrition, HIV infection rates (people with the HIV virus are more likely to get tuberculosis), population movement, and antibiotic resistance. In 1999, at least 8 million people developed active tuberculosis and 2 million died.[10] "We declared victory too soon," said Helene Gayle of the Centers for Disease Control and Prevention.[11]

Tuberculosis is caused by *Mycobacterium tuberculosis,* a bacillus (rod-shaped bacterium) that gets into the lungs and lymphatic system, where it attracts white blood cells and forms growths called tubercles. Over time, the disease can spread to other parts of the body. Symptoms include cough, fever, and weight loss. If not treated, each person with active tuberculosis could infect between ten and fifteen people a year.[12]

One out of every three people in the world is already infected with *Mycobacterium tuberculosis* (in Asia, it is one out of two).[13] In healthy people, tuberculosis usually remains dormant—the immune system walls off the bacilli, where it can remain dormant for years and years. Only about 2 percent of infected people will eventually become sick with active tuberculosis. But people whose immune systems are weakened are more likely to get active tuberculosis.

The global tuberculosis epidemic is growing. Every second a new person is infected somewhere in the world. The disease is spreading into wealthier countries with the arrival of immigrants from areas where tuberculosis is widespread. The World Health Organization estimates that an additional one billion people will become infected, 200 million people will become sick, and 35 million will die between the years 2000 and 2020, unless additional measures are taken.[14]

About 15 percent of people who get treated for tuberculosis will die. For those who get no treatment, half will not survive.[15] Until fifty years ago, there were no drugs to treat tuberculosis. Now there are a variety of drugs, but many of them are useless due to antibiotic resistance. One of the reasons tuberculosis has become resistant to antibiotics is that many people stop taking the drugs before the disease is cured.

Tuberculosis treatment can take up to a year or more. Patients, particularly if they are homeless or have limited access to medical care, often stop taking

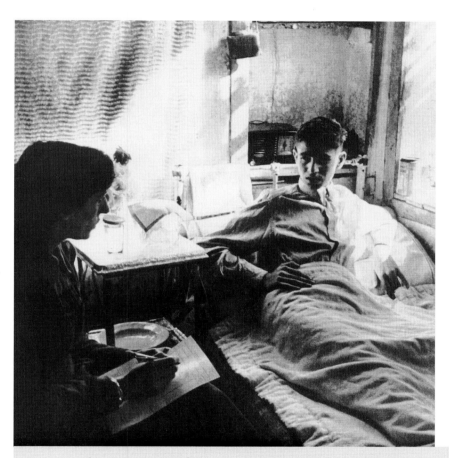

Antibiotics gave new hope to tuberculosis patients in the years after World War II. Unfortunately, drug resistance has become a major roadblock in treating this difficult disease.

the antibiotics early, allowing resistant organisms to survive and be passed on to other victims.

Up until recently, cases of drug-resistant tuberculosis developed within patients' bodies as a result of their not using antibiotics properly. Now, doctors are seeing cases of drug-resistant tuberculosis in newly infected patients. This means that drug-resistant strains are spreading. The problem is especially bad in certain "hot spots," such as Estonia (a country in northeastern Europe), where about 40 percent of new cases are resistant to at least one drug. Strangely enough, drug-resistant tuberculosis is not a major problem in Africa. Although tuberculosis is common in the region, few patients get treatment. People who never get treated are less likely to develop drug-resistant tuberculosis than those who get some treatment but are not cured.

The World Health Organization estimates that about 11 percent of all tuberculosis cases are somewhat resistant to the standard drugs used to treat the disease. About one percent of cases are resistant to two or more drugs.[16] At least one hundred countries around the world have drug-resistant strains of tuberculosis in their populations. In China and Eastern Europe, 30 to 40 percent of all new cases of tuberculosis are resistant to at least one antibiotic.

The spread of drug-resistant tuberculosis is a major concern. Unlike AIDS, which requires sexual or blood contact, or malaria, which requires a bite from an infected mosquito, tuberculosis is spread through the air. A cough or sneeze from an infected person releases droplets into the air that can infect people nearby. For this reason, travelers who frequently spend time on airplanes, particularly overseas flights, may be at risk for tuberculosis. Being closed up in a relatively small area with over one hundred people makes it relatively easy to get the disease if someone onboard is an active carrier.

The death rates for multi-drug-resistant tuberculosis are up to thirty times higher than those for drug-susceptible tuberculosis.[17] In the early 1990s, a multiple-drug-resistant strain of tuberculosis killed five hundred people (most of them AIDS patients) in New York City. Curing a case of drug-resistant tuberculosis can involve $10,000 worth of drugs, lengthy hospitalizations, lab work, outpatient care, and even lung surgery, resulting in bills in the hundreds of thousands of dollars.[18]

To help fight the tuberculosis epidemic, the World Health Organization promotes a program called DOTS (Directly Observed Treatment, Short-course). An important part of the program is that community workers and trained volunteers make sure patients take the right drugs, at the right doses, for the right amount of time. The program produces a cure rate of 95 percent. The organization's goal is to detect 70 percent of all new infectious tuberculosis cases and to cure 85 percent of them.

3

Magic Bullets: Antibiotics as Miracle Drugs

The best prescription is knowledge.

—Former Surgeon General of the United States, C. Everett Koop, on his Web site "drkoop.com"

Until relatively recent times, one of two things would happen to someone with a bacterial infection. Either the body's immune system would eventually win out or the person would die. An ear infection could easily last for months, causing terrible pain. Pus (a yellowish fluid produced during an infection) might drain out of the ear as the immune system tried desperately to get rid of the bacteria. The infection could spread from the inner ear into the

34

brain, which usually meant death. People could and did die from paper cuts, scraped knees, and infected toenails. Strep throat could be a fatal disease. Once a dangerous infection took hold, there was nothing a doctor could do. Antibiotics were the miracle drugs that made these horrors ancient history.

The World of Bacteria and Viruses

There are two main agents of disease: bacteria and viruses. Bacteria are microscopic one-celled organisms that are common nearly everywhere. In fact, the average person has one hundred thousand billion bacteria living on his or her skin and in the gut.[1] This makes bacteria a major part of the human body.

Some bacteria are helpful. For example, bacteria break down dead plant and animal tissue, cleaning the environment and producing fertilizer. Bacteria even help clean up toxic waste. For example, scientists used "oil-eating" bacteria to help clean up the spill from the leaking Exxon Valdez oil tanker in Alaska.[2]

Bacteria have varying needs. Some must have air to survive while others can only live in places where no air exists (inside a sealed can of food, for example). Still others thrive in the digestive systems of animals (including humans), despite the powerful acids found there.

Most bacteria are harmless to humans. But some are dangerous—even deadly—to humans or other animals. These are called pathogenic bacteria, or pathogens. If one of these pathogens is not fought off by the body's immune system, slowed by competition from other bacteria, or stopped by antibiotic drugs, it is able to reproduce quickly. Symptoms such as fever, swelling, pain, and vomiting tell people that something is wrong with their health. At this point, the body is suffering from a bacterial infection. Common infections caused by bacteria include ear, sinus, throat (strep throat), and skin infections. But a single bacterium cannot do any damage. It takes tens of thousands or even millions of bacteria working together (producing toxins that cause disease or digesting body tissue) to harm a human body. For example, a child's ear infection may be the work of as many as 20 million bacteria.[3]

Bacteria can cause different problems depending upon where they settle. *Staphylococcus aureus*, for example, will cause "blood poisoning" (septicemia) if it infects the blood, but causes boils (large, painful pimples) if it infects the skin. *Streptococcus pneumoniae* causes pneumonia (a lung infection) but is a common cause of ear infections as well. And just to complicate matters, bacteria may be harmless to humans but harmful to other animals or plants (or vice versa). For example, *Salmonella typhi* causes the deadly typhoid fever in humans but is completely harmless to other animals. *Actinobacillus pleuropneumoniae* causes pneumonia in pigs but is harmless to humans.

Viruses, infectious particles that are much smaller than bacteria, must live and reproduce inside living cells. Doctors have found the battle against viruses even more difficult than the fight against bacteria.

In most cases, even today, people are told to just "wait it out." The common cold, influenza (flu), and varicella (chicken pox) are examples of common viruses. Other viruses, such as the human immuno-deficiency virus (HIV) that causes AIDS, are much more serious. Fortunately, scientists have developed effective vaccines for some viral diseases (such as chicken pox). In recent years, they have also developed medications for treating viral diseases. These antiviral drugs help reduce the severity of viral infections but are not magic bullets that provide a quick cure.

The Invention of Antibiotics

In 1888, German scientist E. de Freudenreich was experimenting with an organism known as the blue-pus bacterium. *Bacillus pyocyaneus* (now known as *Pseudomonas aeruginosa*) produced a blue solution that de Freudenreich noticed stopped the growth of other bacteria in the test tube. The substance, later named pyocyanase, was the first natural antibiotic product (one not made by chemists) to be discovered. Pyocyanase not only stopped some bacteria from growing; it actually killed some of the most danger-ous bacteria of the day, including those causing typhoid fever, anthrax, diphtheria, plague, and skin infections. Pyocyanase was a major breakthrough, but there is a reason it never became the perfect cure for bacterial infections. It turned out to be toxic and unstable. Its only worth was as a skin ointment, and even that use ended by 1913. But pyocyanase opened the door to the possibility that there could be substances, perhaps even produced by bacteria themselves, that could kill dangerous bacteria and save lives.

Around 1905, Paul Ehrlich (1854–1915), a chemist working in Germany, became convinced that a "magic bullet" existed that could kill bacteria without harming its human host. His research led to the development of Salvarsan, a dye linked to arsenic. Salvarsan proved to be an effective antibacterial. Severe side effects limited its use, but it launched new interest in the search for bacteria-killing drugs.[4] Although scientists discovered additional substances that could kill bacteria on surfaces (such as surgical instruments), most were too toxic to apply to human skin and none were safe enough to take internally. The search continued.

In 1928, Alexander Fleming (1881–1955), a Scottish scientist, made a remarkable discovery. He had left a test plate containing *Staphylococcus* bacteria out in the open. He later found that it had been contaminated with a fungus. But remarkably, the mold had wiped out part of the colony of *Staphylococcus*. He realized that the fungus, which turned out to be *Penicillium notatum*, was producing a substance that could kill bacteria. He named the substance penicillin.[5]

Unfortunately, getting penicillin from what Fleming called "mold juice" proved difficult and it led Fleming to doubt it would ever have practical value. Most people agreed—penicillin had no real future. It would be no more successful than the many other attempts at antibacterial drugs had been.

In 1932, German biochemist Gerhard Domagk (1895-1964) discovered that a dye, Prontosil red, was effective against streptococcal infections. He won the Nobel Prize for this discovery in 1939, although it turned out that it was not the dye itself that stopped the infection. The liver changes Prontosil red into two compounds. One of these is sulphanilamide, which kills bacteria. This was the first of the sulfa drugs. Sulfa drugs became early weapons against bacterial infections. Unfortunately, they worked against only a few species of bacteria and bacteria developed resistance to them very quickly. Sulfa drugs also made it more difficult for the body's natural defenses to fight off an infection on its own.

Then came World War II. Governments were frantic to find a way to treat battlefield wound infections, a major cause of death among soldiers. Sulfa drugs helped, but they needed something more.

Not everyone had given up on penicillin. In 1939, researchers Howard Florey and Ernst Chain had set up a system for growing enough mold to treat a human patient. (Both Fleming and Florey had used animals to test the safety of penicillin before trying it on humans.) A forty-three-year-old policeman became their test case to see whether penicillin could cure bacterial infections. The policeman was suffering from an infection that had spread to his eyes, bones, and lungs. All other treatments had failed and it seemed he would die. Florey and his team gave the

Before antibiotics, infection was a major of cause of death. These World War I soldiers could very well have died if their wounds had become infected.

man injections of penicillin. Miraculously, the infection seemed to disappear in a matter of days. But the penicillin was in such short supply that they began to run out. At one point, Florey was forced to filter the man's urine, separating out the penicillin that had passed through his body. This he later injected back into the patient, in one of history's oddest recycling projects. But before long, even that was not enough and there was no more penicillin. The infection surged back as the remaining bacteria (the ones strong enough to resist the initial attack) multiplied. The man died. Fortunately, other, more successful cases followed. Florey and Chain had proven that penicillin did have medical value. They had also shown that if antibiotics were stopped too soon, the organisms that survived would multiply, with tragic results.[6]

The government classified penicillin research as secret in 1942. It was considered a military project of high value. The governments of England and the United States pushed to produce large amounts of penicillin. What was really needed, however, was an understanding of the chemical structure of penicillin so that researchers could synthesize it (assemble it in the laboratory) rather than have to produce it through natural processes. At one point, thirty-nine different laboratories and at least one thousand chemists were trying to synthesize penicillin. According to John C. Sheehan, the man who eventually got the patent for semisynthetic penicillins, "Only the Manhattan Project leading to the development of the atomic bomb equaled the efforts of the Office of Scientific Research and Development during World War II to produce a synthetic penicillin."[7] Despite the massive effort, the project failed.

Then on November 28, 1942, something happened that proved the value of penicillin and the need to produce it in large quantities. On that evening, hundreds, perhaps even a thousand people, jammed the popular Cocoanut Grove nightclub in Boston. Suddenly, fire broke out and the crowd panicked. People pushed toward the single revolving door that led to safety, crushing and suffocating those ahead of them. The fire raged with hundreds trapped inside. More than four hundred people died and more than two hundred were rushed to area hospitals, burned but still alive. Doctors knew their chances for survival were not good. Burn victims are frequent targets for bacteria, which easily enter the large areas of broken skin and cause deadly blood infections. There was nothing available to fight the bacteria that caused these infections. Suddenly, a secret weapon was brought in. It came with police escorts, traveling 368 miles through four states. Newspapers described the drug as "priceless" and said that it was being used as a "medical safeguard against infection." Although it was still a closely guarded secret and was reserved for use only by the military, officials had made an exception and let the victims of the Cocoanut Grove fire have penicillin. Their action saved countless lives. But it also spurred the government to back large-scale production of penicillin.[8]

By the mid-1940s, scientists learned how to produce penicillin in larger quantities and the drug was released to the public on June 1, 1946. Newspapers and magazines described penicillin as a miracle drug. There were amazing success stories. But even with all the excitement, there was a word of caution. Alexander Fleming, the man who had discovered penicillin, warned that extensive use of the miracle drug could cause bacteria to grow resistant to penicillin. He even predicted that the situation would get worse when the drug became available as a pill and people could take it themselves.[9] How right he was.

Selman Waksman (1888–1973) approached

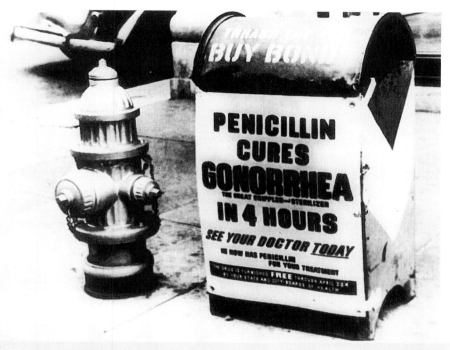

Penicillin was hailed as a miracle drug when it was first released to the public after World War II.

antibiotics in a down-to-earth manner. He decided to study *Streptomyces*, a bacteria family that is common in soil. He reasoned that soil must be loaded with antibiotics or Earth would be overrun with bacteria. His biggest success was streptomycin, from *Streptomyces griseus*, which became a popular drug for treating tuberculosis as well as many other types of infections.[10] Finally, antibiotics were changing the odds in the war between humans and bacteria. By 1954, 2 million pounds of antibiotics were being produced in the United States each year.[11]

How Antibiotics Work

There are two types of antibiotics. One, which is called bactericidal, kills bacteria. The other, called bacteriostatic, inhibits the growth of bacteria. A good antibiotic is like a bacteria-seeking missile. It targets a type of bacteria, finds it, and kills it or stops its growth without harming the host.

Antibiotics approach their jobs differently. Some, such as penicillin and cephalosporin, break down the cell walls of the bacteria. (Human cells do not have

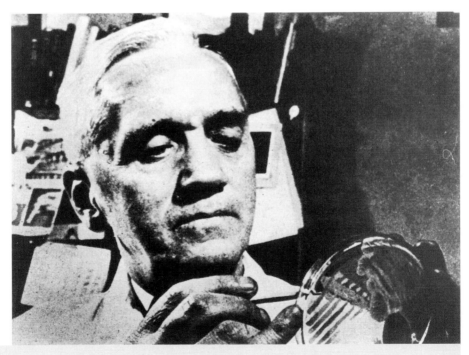

Alexander Fleming discovered the miracle drug penicillin in 1928. But even he foresaw the dangers of antibiotic resistance.

walls, so healthy tissue is not harmed.) Others, such as streptomycin and rifampicin, a drug used to treat tuberculosis, hurt the bacteria's ability to make proteins, which they need to survive. Sulfa drugs take the place of a chemical the bacteria need. By doing this, they prevent the bacteria from getting a vital ingredient.

There are now more than one hundred fifty different antibiotics in use.[12] So how do doctors choose which one to give a patient? Some antibiotics are broad spectrum—they kill a wide variety of bacteria. These are somewhat like hand grenades. When they explode, they take out pretty much everything around them. When doctors know the kind of bacteria that are causing the problem, they can use more precise weapons called narrow-spectrum antibiotics that target specific bacteria.

When doctors want to know which type of bacteria is causing the problem, they take a specimen (blood, urine, stool, skin cells, etc.) from the patient and send it to a laboratory. Technicians place the specimen in a test tube or bottle filled with broth or with other nutrient-rich material that favors the growth of bacteria. After giving the bacteria a chance to grow, the technicians use a metal wand to spread a small amount of the solution on a small plastic plate containing a jelly-like nutrient mix (agar and other ingredients). Bacteria in the solution grow and form colonies, groups containing so many bacteria that they can be seen by the naked eye. Technicians examining the plates can identify the bacteria (using a microscope) and report how many of which type are present. This process, developed by Robert Koch in 1881, helps identify which bacteria are causing the problem. Sometimes doctors can use screening tests, such as the test for strep throat, that let them know immediately whether *Streptococcus* bacteria are present on a throat swab.

Susceptibility tests determine which antibiotics the bacteria are susceptible to (which ones will kill or inhibit the bacteria). When the bacteria have grown

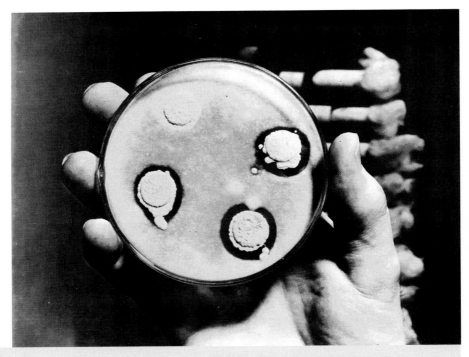

Disks containing antibiotics are placed on plates containing bacterial cultures. A clear ring around the disk indicates that the drug has killed the bacteria. No ring indicates that the bacteria are resistant to that antibiotic.

into colonies that can be seen with the naked eye, discs containing different antibiotics are dropped onto the plate. After a day, the technician checks the plate. If there is a large, clear ring around a disc (where before bacteria were thriving), the antibiotic has killed or inhibited all the bacteria around it. The technician will report that the bacteria are susceptible to that antibiotic. If bacteria are still growing right up to the edge of a disc, it means the antibiotic is having no effect on them. The technician will report that the bacteria are resistant to that antibiotic. The report goes back to the doctor, who can then choose an antibiotic that will be effective. These susceptibility tests are the only sure way to know which antibiotic has the best chance of curing a particular infection. Of course, in the case of severely ill patients, doctors cannot wait for test results and often begin antibiotic treatment immediately. They usually choose a broad-spectrum antibiotic that will work against many kinds of bacteria, or make an educated guess based upon which bacteria they think are to blame.

4

Antibiotics: Too Much of a Good Thing?

Nothing is more fatal to health than an overcare of it.

—Benjamin Franklin

It is difficult for a modern-day American to imagine what life would be like without antibiotics. Each year in the United States, drug manufacturers produce 50 million pounds of antibiotics. Humans consume 235 million doses of antibiotics a year.[1] Children are some of the heaviest antibiotic users. Antibiotic use among children jumped more than 48 percent between 1980 and 1999.[2] More antibiotics are prescribed for kids' ear infections than for anything else. Prescriptions for antibiotics to treat middle ear infections rose from 15 million in 1985 to 23.6 million in 1992.[3] This dependence on antibiotics is at the root of the problem of drug-resistant diseases.

Growing Reliance on Antibiotics

Antibiotics are used to treat a wide variety of ailments. But 30 to 50 percent of all antibiotics used in the United States are given not to cure disease but to prevent it.[4] Antibiotics cannot keep bacteria from getting into the body, but they can stop bacteria from establishing large populations. For this reason, doctors often give antibiotics to people they know will be exposed to disease-causing bacteria and will need help keeping them under control. For example, people undergoing certain types of surgery have a higher risk of infection. To help prevent infection, doctors often start these surgical patients on antibiotics before the operation.

In addition to the antibiotic drugs used to treat bacterial infections inside the body, people use a variety of antibacterial products to kill bacteria on surfaces or in water. Antibacterials are used in hospitals, homes, schools, restaurants, farms, food processing plants, water treatment facilities, and other places. According to the Environmental Protection Agency (EPA), for disinfectants alone, 3.3 billion pounds of active ingredients were produced in 1995.[5] Worldwide, the market for antibacterial products is estimated at $25 billion.[6]

Companies know that people are concerned about reducing the spread of disease, so they have created an amazing array of products to meet this real or imagined need. In Japan, where concern for cleanliness has reached frantic levels, people can buy antibacterial pencils, floppy disks, refrigerators, pillows, and even socks and underwear. In the United States, the Soap and Detergent Association estimates that $630 million worth of antibacterial products were sold in 1998.[7]

Some scientists say that all these antibacterial soaps, detergents, household cleaners, disinfectants, antiseptics, and even the chlorine people put in swimming pools to kill bacteria, actually add to the growth of drug-resistant bacteria. For example, one study showed that chlorinated river water contains more bacteria that are resistant to streptomycin than river water that has not been chlorinated.[8]

The Soap and Detergent Association emphasizes that antibacterial wash products have been used for over

Zithromax, manufactured by Pfizer, Inc., is a brand-name antibiotic that is often prescribed in the United States.

Antibacterial soaps and detergents meant to reduce the spread of disease are now widely marketed. But some scientists believe these products add to the growth of drug-resistant disease.

thirty years (they were first used to control odor-causing bacteria). They say that during that time there has been no evidence of a direct link between antibacterial use and antibiotic-resistant bacteria. In fact, they argue that the use of antibacterial products can help to kill resistant bacteria.

Nevertheless, some people question the need for bacteria-killing chemicals in so many consumer products and wonder whether use of these products simply gives bacteria a better chance to get to know and learn how to defeat the enemy. They point to the fact that some strains of *Escherichia coli* (an organism

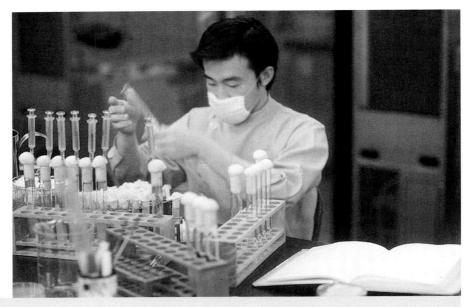

A researcher in Japan screens soil for bacteria.

that can cause diarrhea) resist triclosan, an antiseptic used in many antibacterial soaps and toothpaste products. They say this is evidence that antibacterial products simply create more problems.

Do we really need antibacterial substances in cat litter? Plastic toys? Ballpoint pens? The manufacturers say that people want and buy the products and that they are safe.

Despite all the modern "magic bullets," the oceans of antibacterial washes, and advances such as vaccines and high-tech laboratory tests, deaths from infectious diseases are rising. Between 1980 and 1992, deaths from infectious disease in the United States rose 58 percent.[9] Part of the increase is due to an aging population, AIDS, and other causes. But a significant number of these deaths occurred because once-effective drugs are no longer able to beat the bacteria.

Overuse and Misuse of Antibiotics

The Centers for Disease Control and Prevention (CDC) estimates that doctors in American medical offices order about 100 million courses of antibiotics each year. A course of antibiotics means a full period of treatment, often ten days. About half of these are unnecessary.[10] In many cases, the prescriptions are not necessary because the patient has a viral infection such as a cold that is not affected by antibiotics. As an old saying explains: "An untreated cold goes on for seven days; a treated cold lasts a week."

Sometimes doctors prescribe antibiotics because they are guessing that the patient has a bacterial infection. Other times, they are trying to prevent secondary infections (an infection that sets in while the body is fighting off a virus). And sometimes they prescribe antibiotics simply because that is what patients want. Sick people and worried parents pressure doctors to "do something." They do not want to hear that they should just go home and wait for the viral infection to burn itself out. As Surgeon General David Satcher told a Senate subcommittee on public health and safety, "People often just feel better when they get medication."[11]

Parents often pressure doctors to prescribe antibiotics when their children are sick. One study of six hundred pediatricians found that 96 percent of doctors surveyed reported that parents had recently requested antibiotics for their children in cases where they were not needed. One third of the doctors admitted to giving the parents the antibiotics. "Doctors need to do two things," says Bernadette Albanese, a pediatric infectious disease specialist. "They need to stand their ground when an antibiotic is not needed. But they also have a responsibility to explain to the patient why an antibiotic isn't necessary and to give them some tips on how to take care of their symptoms."[12]

Drugs for Viruses

Viruses can be more difficult to treat than bacteria because they grow and reproduce inside the body's cells, where it is difficult to get at them. For some viruses, scientists have had luck developing vaccines to prevent the viruses from getting established. In other cases, doctors have had to rely on antiviral drugs (drugs that kill viruses), which have limited effectiveness and suffer from some of the same resistance problems as antibiotics.

One of the biggest health concerns in modern times is AIDS, a condition in which the patient's immune system has been severely damaged. AIDS patients are open to attack by organisms that would be easily fought off by a healthy person with a normal immune system. AIDS is caused by the human immunodeficiency virus (HIV). Until an effective vaccine is developed, doctors are trying to keep patients alive using a variety of drugs designed to keep the HIV at low levels. This delays the development of AIDS. Unfortunately, patients do not always respond well to the drugs, or they sometimes experience a "rebound" effect. Rebounds occur when HIV levels rise after initially being lowered by the medication. Some of the rebound effect is due to patients not taking their drugs properly or to their bodies losing the ability to use the medicines effectively. But the HIV virus has also developed resistance to many of the drugs.

At a conference in February 1999, researchers

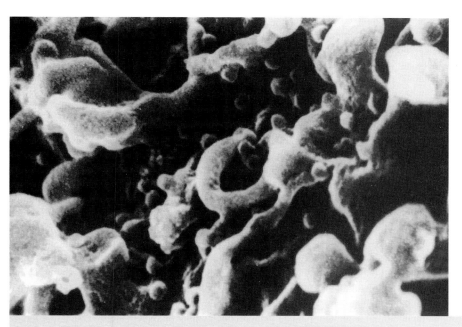

This is a microscopic view of human immunodeficiency virus, or HIV, the virus that causes AIDS. HIV is becoming increasingly resistant to drug treatments.

reported on a study that found that the rate of resistance was growing much more quickly than expected, at a rate considered alarming. In some cities, scientists reported more than one in four new HIV infections involved drug-resistant viruses. Dr. John W. Mellors, professor of infectious diseases at the University of Pittsburgh, said: "Drug resistance is a big problem, and it's not going away."[13]

In September 1999, three different research teams reported they had found that multi-drug-resistant strains of HIV were spreading in the United States and Europe. "These are not wimpy viruses that cannot be transmitted," said Dr. Martin Markowitz of

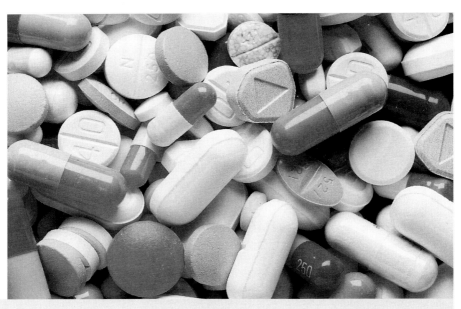

Sometimes a disease is helped by a combination of pills. New drugs to treat disease are constantly being developed.

the Aaron Diamond AIDS Research Center in New York City. "From a public health point of view it means we need to identify drug-resistant cases early."[14]

Doctors have turned to testing patient's blood samples to measure the levels of resistance in the particular virus they are carrying. By determining the drug resistance, the doctor can prescribe a mixture of drugs more likely to successfully attack that specific virus. Patients with HIV are often treated with "cocktails," mixtures of drugs, to increase the chances of success. In the past, if the patient did not show significant improvement, all the drugs in the mix were stopped. With testing, doctors may find that one of the drugs is still effective, while others in the mix are not. One study found that 51 percent of patients who received drugs based on the results of such testing had favorable responses, as opposed to 25 percent of those who did not have the benefit of resistance testing.[15]

The testing is not perfect. Some patients carry more than one strain of HIV. Testing may miss strains that are at low levels in the blood. Tests are expensive and take time. HIV has a great ability to change; so keeping up with current resistance could be tricky. Still, researchers were encouraged by the early results.

Antibiotic Resistance Around the World

In 1981, the Indonesian Ministry of Religion was preparing for a mass pilgrimage. One hundred thousand people would be traveling from Indonesia to Saudi Arabia on a trip to the religious center, Mecca. The ministry knew that many lives had been lost to infectious diseases on past trips, due to the close contact and the contaminated food and water. They particularly feared cholera. After checking all foods that would be served on the trains and planes, and testing every participant for cholera, they took one additional step. They gave every traveler a seven-day dose of the antibiotic tetracycline, the drug of choice for treating cholera. The drug, which was reportedly "dished out of vats like coffee beans," had not even been tested to be sure that the drug was fully active. According to Stuart B. Levy, an expert on antibiotic resistance, such practices contributed to the development of tetracycline-resistant strains of *Vibrio cholerae*, the organism that causes cholera. In some parts of Africa, over 50 percent of cholera strains are now resistant to tetracycline.[16]

The problem of antibiotic resistance is complicated by government policies, particularly in developing countries. In Mexico, the Caribbean, Southeast Asia, and many South and Central American countries, for example, people can get antibiotics from drug stores. They do not even need a prescription or doctor's order. In these areas, healthy people often take these drugs thinking they will help them ward off infections. They do not realize that they are doing themselves—and others—more harm than good. In some cases, people who took antibiotics over long periods of time developed such highly resistant infections when they did get sick that they died before their infections could be controlled.

Another problem that can lead to drug resistance is that in other parts of the world antibiotics may be manufactured incorrectly. Locally made cheaper versions of common antibiotics may not be full strength. They may be made to look like commercial antibiotics, but be watered-down versions of the real thing.

Governments of developing countries are also faced with limited budgets. As a result, clinics may give patients shorter courses of treatment or smaller doses of antibiotics. This not only allows the infection to continue, but also increases the likelihood that it will be passed to others. It also raises the odds that the disease-causing organism will develop drug resistance. In a study in Vietnam, researchers found that over 70 percent of patients were given doses that were too low.[17] Whenever patients take antibiotics in lower than effective doses, the result is to encourage the development of drug-resistant bacteria. Inadequate treatment with an antibiotic is often worse than none because that kind of treatment allows the worst bacteria to survive while killing the less dangerous strains that would have competed with the more harmful strains.

The Cost of Antibiotic Resistance

It is difficult to estimate the actual cost of drug-resistant disease, either in terms of money or loss of life. The problem causes longer hospital stays, increased drug costs, higher insurance rates, loss of work days, increased need for health care workers, and more spending for research and development of new treatments. For these reasons, studies indicate that the total cost of antibiotic resistance may be as high as $3 billion per year in the United States.[18]

In terms of financial cost, one report estimated the cost of antibiotic resistance for a single organism (*Staphylococcus aureus*) was $122 million a year.[19] The Centers for Disease Control and Prevention (CDC) estimates that hospital-acquired infections result in patient care costs of $3.5 billion per year.[20] One reason for the increased cost is that when common antibiotics fail, newer, more expensive medicines must be used. Some of the drugs cost over five hundred dollars a day as compared to older forms of penicillin that cost less than a dollar a day.

The National Institute of Allergy and Infectious Diseases in Bethesda, Maryland, estimates that cases of drug-resistant tuberculosis are one hundred times more expensive to treat than cases of drug-sensitive tuberculosis.[21] The cost of curing a single case of multiple-drug-resistant tuberculosis can be as high as $250,000. The cost of battling outbreaks is even higher. An epidemic of multiple-drug-resistant tuberculosis that killed five hundred people in New York in the early 1990s cost $1 billion to stop.[22]

Due to concern about the rise in cases of drug-resistant tuberculosis, the National Institute of Allergy and Infectious Diseases in the United States increased its budget for tuberculosis research to $42.5 million in 2000, more than fifteen times the amount spent ten years earlier. The United States has also stepped up its aid to other countries, recently doubling its foreign grants for tuberculosis control to $22 million.

It is difficult to measure the impact of drug-resistant disease on human health. In some cases, it may just be that an ear infection takes a few extra weeks to cure or a patient may have to stay in the hospital a few days longer. In others, a severely ill patient may die before doctors can find the right antibiotic. For patients with life-threatening infections, doctors may have only one shot at choosing an antibiotic that will do the job. If the first antibiotic is one that the bacteria are able to resist, the patient may not get a second chance. These cases may or may not ever get counted as cases of drug-resistant disease because it is difficult to say whether or not the patient might have died anyway. In developing countries, patients may not have access to new or expensive drugs for fighting antibiotic-resistant diseases. Government health organizations may not be able to afford the new, powerful drugs manufactured by companies in wealthier countries.

5

Antibiotics and Food

We are the microbes, my friend
And we'll keep dividing
Till the end
We are the microbes
We are the microbes
No time for chlorine
Cause we are the microbes in your food

—Excerpt from "We Are the Microbes" (song to the tune of "We Are the Champions" by Queen) by Dr. Carl Winter, extension food toxicologist, director, FoodSafe Program, University of California, Davis, California

In 1999, when a 66-year-old woman near Detroit developed a serious infection after heart surgery, doctors felt confident giving her Synercid. Synercid is a powerful antibiotic that had only just been released in the fall. But they were shocked to find that the bacteria causing the woman's infection were already resistant to the new drug. As a result, the patient died.[1]

Some researchers say that the rapid growth in resistance to Synercid is due to the use of a closely related drug, Virginiamycin, in food animals. One study found Virginiamycin-resistant bacteria in as much as 50 percent of the supermarket chicken, turkey, and pork tested. It is difficult to prove that the use of Virginiamycin in animals led directly to resistance problems with Synercid. Nevertheless, many experts believe that human exposure to antibiotics in food, water, and other sources contributes to the problem of drug-resistant diseases.

Antibiotics in Feed for Food Animals

More than 40 percent of the antibiotics made in the United States are not given to people; they are given to animals.[2] Some of these antibiotics are used to treat infections, but farmers and food production companies also put antibiotics in animal feed to boost growth. Currently, about thirty antibiotics are approved by the United States government for use in food animals such as cattle (used for beef and to produce milk), hogs (used for pork), and poultry (chickens, turkeys, and other edible birds). Some of these drugs are no different from the medicines doctors prescribe for ear infections and other human diseases: penicillin, streptomycin, and tetracycline.

But food producers use constant, small doses (usually less than two ounces of drug in a ton of feed).[3]

These small doses kill off bacteria that would normally be killed by the animal's immune system. This saves the animal energy, allowing it to grow more quickly. In addition, when the immune system is fighting bacteria, it releases chemicals that make the animal have less of an appetite. With antibiotics doing the work, the animals have bigger appetites, eat more, and therefore grow faster. But those small amounts of antibiotics add up. Each year, 20 million pounds of antibiotics are given to animals, not to cure infections but to make them grow faster and produce more meat.[4]

People have been concerned about the use of antibiotics in animal feed for some time. In 1978, the Food and Drug Administration proposed removing penicillin and tetracycline from the list of antibiotics approved for uses other than to treat disease. Congress did not approve the request, pointing to a review by the National Academy of Sciences that found the risks to human health were "neither proven nor disproven."[5]

Many scientists think that the use of antibiotics in animal feed contributes to the problem of drug-resistant diseases in humans. A particular concern is a veterinary antibiotic, avoparcin. This antibiotic resembles vancomycin, the drug that is often the last line of defense against drug-resistant infections in humans. Organisms that are resistant to avoparcin are likely to be resistant to vancomycin as well. In Germany, researchers found vancomycin-resistant

Enterococci in meat and meat products. Meat from organic farms, which do not use antibiotics, did not contain this strain.[6]

Some say that for this reason, antibiotics that are similar to those used for humans should not be given to animals. "It's clear that the use of Virginiamycin to promote the growth of food animals is a hazard to human health," says Frederick J. Angulo of the Centers for Disease Control and Prevention. Others disagree. "We're not at all convinced, based on the data, that Virginiamycin is the cause of the Synercid resistance, however minimal, in the human population," said Carl Johnson of Pfizer, Inc., the company that developed Virginiamycin. He believes the resistance is coming from hospital use of Synercid.[7]

A 1999 outbreak of drug-resistant salmonella in Denmark sickened twenty-seven people. Two of these people died. The cause was meat from infected pigs, but the real concern was that the organism had partial resistance to a class of antibiotics known as fluoroquinolones. These drugs are among the most powerful weapons doctors have for severe cases of *Salmonella*. In Denmark, fluoroquinolones are also used to treat some illnesses in pigs. As a result, some researchers think that the use of the antibiotics in pigs may have produced drug-resistant *Salmonella* bacteria, which then entered the food supply. "Fluoroquinolones become a drug of last resort for some of these infections," said Levy. "If we're beginning to lose these drugs, where do we go from here?"[8]

In response to concerns, the Food and Drug

Administration proposed new guidelines to limit the spread of antibiotic resistance. Administration officials said they would begin making drug companies prove that any new animal antibiotics would not increase antibiotic resistance in humans. In addition, they said they would review some existing animal antibiotics.

Drug companies and livestock producers have protested the actions. They say the new requirements are unnecessary and may make food less safe from disease-causing organisms. Without antibiotics, sick animals may enter the food supply, they warn.

Mark E. Cook, an animal scientist at the University of Wisconsin at Madison, has developed an alternative to feeding antibiotics to chickens. Cook found that antibiotics do not directly increase an animal's growth. What they do is stop the immune system from releasing chemicals that reduce the animal's appetite when fighting disease. Cook has been able to create a substance that blocks the appetite-reducing chemicals without hurting the chicken's ability to battle disease. When the substance is added to chicken feed, the birds eat more and grow faster, without the use of antibiotics.[9]

Arguments over the use of antibiotics in food animals continue. J. Glenn Morris of the University of Maryland in Baltimore says: "The Synercid story is just starting to play out. We know we have a major problem on our hands in terms of antibiotic resistance in our hospitals. The question about Synercid is whether we'll act to protect it now, or just accept the risk that it and other important antibiotics may become ineffective sooner because of this animal use."[10]

The Bellyache Makers: Food-borne Bacteria

Each year, several thousand people are made ill by organisms that cause what is commonly called food poisoning. Food poisoning is actually not poisoning at all, but an infection caused by food-borne bacteria. It occurs when someone eats or drinks substances that contain certain disease-causing organisms. These illnesses normally cause vomiting, diarrhea, and other intestinal problems. In elderly people and young children, however, food-borne bacteria can cause serious infections or even death. This is because their immune systems are less able to fight off the bacteria.

One of the most common food-borne bacteria is *Salmonella*, which is commonly found in chicken, turkey, eggs, beef, and other foods from animals. Each year, an estimated 800,000 to 4 million people become sick from *Salmonella* infections. And according to the Centers for Disease Control and Prevention (CDC), each year *Salmonella* organisms are responsible for 8,000 to 18,000 hospitalizations and 500 deaths.

Some strains of *Salmonella* have become resistant to antibiotics. Between 68,000 and 340,000 Americans are sickened by *Salmonella* DT-104 each year. About 95 percent of *Salmonella* DT-104 strains are resistant to five major classes of antibiotics. In recent years, a strain of *Salmonella typhimurium* has

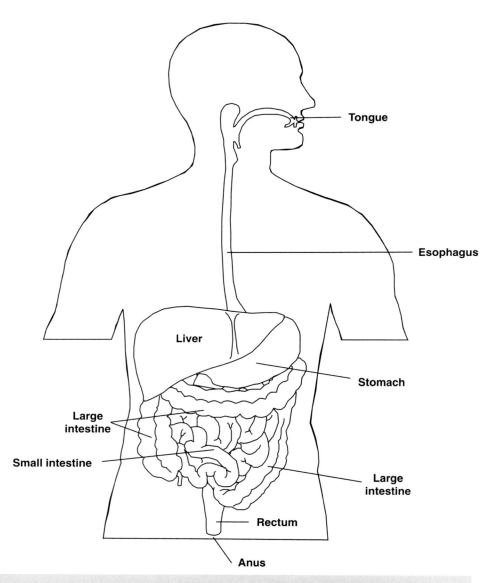

Tongue

Esophagus

Liver

Stomach

Large intestine

Small intestine

Large intestine

Rectum

Anus

Food-borne infections occur when someone eats or drinks something containing disease-causing organisms. We get sick when these microbes reproduce in large numbers.

become resistant to all known antibiotics. The antibiotic-resistant strain can be ten times more deadly than the regular form.

Campylobacter is another organism found in foods of animal origin. Although *Campylobacter jejuni* is not a familiar name to most people, it causes more cases of food-borne illness than any other single organism. Some 2 to 4 million Americans a year suffer *Campylobacter* infections[11] and between 200 and 730 die.[12] The illness is common because most raw poultry sold in the United States is contaminated with the *Campylobacter* organism. *Campylobacter* is also found in pork and beef. Anyone who handles infected meat carelessly or fails to cook it properly can become ill.

According to a study conducted by the Food and Drug Administration, at least five thousand Americans each year suffer longer bouts of food-borne illness due to resistant strains of *Campylobacter* in chicken.[13] *Campylobacter* can also cause long-term problems, such as a form of arthritis (a painful condition of the joints). One in one thousand cases of *Campylobacter* infections result in Guillain-Barré syndrome, a disease that can cause paralysis.

Escherichia coli (E. coli) are rod-shaped bacteria that live in the intestines of all humans and most other animals. Most of the time, they are harmless. If not controlled by the immune system, *E. coli* produces diarrhea and vomiting. This can happen in small children, whose immune systems are not fully developed. It can also happen in any human being if the particular strain of *E. coli* produces especially tough toxins.

In 1982, seemingly from out of nowhere, a new strain showed up: *E. coli* 0157: H7. It produced dangerous hemorrhages (massive bleeding) in the intestinal tract and kidneys of people of any age. In most cases, the source was contaminated meat. And like most strains of *E. coli*, it had become moderately resistant to several antibiotics. In the 1990s, several outbreaks of *E. coli* 0157:H7 caused serious illnesses and deaths. A 1991 outbreak caused serious illness in twenty-seven people. The cause was contaminated apple cider. It turned out that the apple trees had been fertilized with livestock manure that contained *E. coli* 0157:H7. In 1993, more than five hundred people became ill from *E. coli* 0157:H7. They had eaten contaminated hamburgers from Jack-in-the-Box fast-food restaurants in Washington State. Four of them died. As a result, the government ordered increased inspections of meat and consumer groups pushed for restrictions on the use of antibiotics in livestock. Today, the organism continues to be a problem. Each year, fifty to one hundred Americans die from *E. coli* 0157: H7 infections.[14]

Shigella is an organism that can cause shigellosis, a form of food poisoning that causes diarrhea (sometimes bloody), fever, and stomach cramps for one to three days. Young children and elderly patients may become so ill that they require hospitalization. People can become infected not just from contaminated food, but also from contact with an infected person—even one who has no symptoms. People with weakened immune systems, including people with AIDS, are especially at risk.

In the early 1960s, doctors started seeing cases of *Shigella dysenteriae* that were resistant to penicillin. This particularly nasty strain killed up to 20 percent of children and 15 percent of adults when untreated with antibiotics.

In September 1983, a Hopi woman living on her American Indian land in Arizona was hospitalized for *Shigella* dysentery. Doctors found that it was no ordinary *Shigella* strain. The woman had a history of urinary infections and for years had taken several antibiotics on and off to treat them. Her intestines had become a breeding ground where antibiotic-resistant *Shigella* organisms shared their abilities to resist different antibiotics. Even though doctors tried to prevent its spread, the super bug spread and by 1987 was responsible for up to 21 percent of all *Shigella* infections among the Hopi and nearby Navajo.[15]

Drinking contaminated water (or eating food washed in the water) can also cause food-borne illness. Organisms enter the water supply when the waste of infected animals or humans is dumped or washes into the water. The problem of unsafe water is not just a concern in countries with poor sanitation. Water-borne disease-causing organisms have developed an ability to resist the disinfectants and antibacterials such as chlorine that are used to purify the water.

In January 1987, an outbreak of intestinal infections due to *Cryptosporidium* hit Carroll County, Georgia. Out of a population of only 64,900 people,

13,000 became ill within one month. The source was the public water system, even though the water met federal standards for water purification. *Cryptosporidium*, a tiny parasite not much larger than most bacteria, had become resistant to the chlorine disinfectant.[16] A 1993 outbreak in Milwaukee, Wisconsin, affected 400,000 people and killed more than one hundred.[17] A study later showed that the Milwaukee *Cryptosporidium* strain was so resistant to disinfectants that it could actually live in Clorox bleach.

In some cases, water-borne organisms use sporulation to toughen their cell walls and wait until the threat passes. Some microbes are so good at this that they can actually float unharmed in disinfectants designed to kill them. This tactic allows organisms such as cholera to live in water that has been chlorinated in an attempt to make it safe to drink. In other cases, organisms use a pumping technique similar to the one used by bacteria to pump out antibiotics. Governments must add higher levels of chlorine to make the drinking water safe, raising concerns about the dangers of excessive chlorine.

The Natural Resources Defense Council, a citizens action group, reviewed U.S. water systems and found that nearly one million Americans were made ill and 900 were killed each year by contaminated water.[18] A particularly frightening situation occurred in 1993, when tests showed that the deadly organism *E. coli* 0157:H7 had entered the New York City public water supply. This forced thirty-five thousand residents to switch to boiled water as a precaution. Fortunately, quick action prevented a major outbreak. The increasing ability of water-borne disease-causing organisms to resist chlorination and other types of disinfection are a major concern to public health officials.

Other Ways Humans Take in Antibiotics

Some people are concerned about the amount of antibiotic residue and the numbers of antibiotic-resistant organisms in the general environment. Large amounts of antibiotics enter the environment through animal waste. Domestic animals (farm animals and pets) outnumber humans in the United States by more then five to one. Most of the 6 billion animals raised for food and the 100 to 150 million pet cats and dogs are given antibiotics at some point.[19] Commercial producers also give antibiotics to animals such as fox and mink that are raised for their pelts.

Animals that are routinely given antibiotics produce waste that contains bacteria that are antibiotic-resistant. Considering the volume of waste some of these animals produce (a cow produces one hundred times more waste than a human), large numbers of these organisms are entering the environment. The bacteria can then be spread to other areas through contact with animals and humans, transfer by birds or flies, or by ending up in fertilizer for crops.

In a Massachusetts study, a group of month-old chickens on a farm was given feed containing an antibiotic. Within one to two days, stool specimens contained bacteria that were resistant to the antibiotic. Within five to six months, resistant bacteria turned up in the stool samples of the farm workers and the family that lived in the nearby farmhouse, even though they had not taken any antibiotics themselves and had not eaten any of the chickens. Stool specimens taken from people living in the same area (but not on the farm with the chickens) had no resistant bacteria.[20]

Scientists are also concerned about people eating meat that contains antibiotic residues (small amounts of antibiotic left behind). The Food and Drug Administration's Center for Veterinary Medicine limits the amount of antibiotic residue in poultry and other meats, and the United States Department of Agriculture monitors meats for residue. The limits are designed to be low enough so that the amount of antibiotics people take in when they eat the meat will not be large enough to produce resistance in the normal bacteria in their gut. Antibiotic residues can also end up in water. Few studies have been conducted to determine the amount of residue that ends up in the environment or in food or drinking water.

Do not think that antibiotics can be avoided by eating only fish. Much of the fish that appears in stores has been grown on fish farms, commercial ponds designed for raising fish that will later be sold for food. Producers use antibiotics to treat and prevent bacterial infection in fish such as catfish and salmon that people will later eat. Antibiotics are even sold for fish in home aquariums. Tetracycline and erythromycin are only two of the common antibiotics for human use that are commonly sold (with no prescription required) for treating diseases in tropical fish.

Food-borne antibiotics are not just found in meat. Increasingly, food sold in grocery stores has been grown on fish farms. Producers use antibiotics to treat and prevent bacterial infection in fish that people will later eat.

Animals are not even the only ones being fed antibiotics. In the United States alone, forty thousand to fifty thousand pounds of antibiotics are fed each year to fruit trees. Antibiotics are sprayed on fruit trees to control or prevent bacterial infections. Such use can leave antibiotic residues that encourage the growth of resistant bacteria. This residue can end up on the fruit, where it may or may not be washed off before eating. The spray can also drift to other trees, killing off sensitive bacteria and allowing resistant bacteria to grow.[21] Farmers also use antibiotics to treat or prevent bacterial diseases in celery, potatoes, peppers, tomatoes, coconuts, and a variety of other ornamental plants, fruit trees, vegetable plants, and trees. Farmers even give antibiotics to bees that make honey, to prevent and control bacterial infections in beehives.

People who work or live around others who are using antibiotics run a higher risk of getting a drug-resistant infection. This is particularly true of day-care workers, teachers, hospital employees, and people working in doctors' offices because they are in contact with so many sick people every day. But studies have shown that even people who happen to have a family member who is taking an antibiotic have more resistant bacteria in their throats or on their skin. This is particularly true if the person is on

The fight against drug-resistant diseases continues.

long-term antibiotic therapy. People who work on farms where drugs are routinely given to livestock also have increased levels of resistant bacteria. These drug-resistant organisms may not cause problems for the person carrying them, but they can still be spread to others.

6

Doctors Fight Back

One of the first duties of the physician is to educate the masses not to take medicine.

—William Osler,
Canadian physician and author

Years ago, doctors prescribed antibiotics routinely. Even if a patient had only a cold or virus (neither of which is affected by antibiotics), doctors figured it would not hurt. They figured an antibiotic would help if there were an infection in addition to the virus and might help prevent other infections from taking hold. At worst, it was simply a waste of money and effort. Now, doctors are realizing that overuse of antibiotics is at the heart of the drug-resistant disease problem.

Reducing Antibiotic Misuse

Doctors today are learning that there is no benefit to prescribing antibiotics unnecessarily. They are also learning that unnecessary prescriptions of antibiotics carry a risk. Complicating this picture is the pressure to reduce medical costs. HMOs and other health management systems pay doctors a fixed amount per patient per month for all their office visits and care. Additional patient visits cost the doctor money. As a result, doctors are more likely to prescribe an antibiotic (sometimes even over the phone) in an effort to quickly solve the problem. For this reason, poor patients, who generally see doctors less often, are actually less likely to get a resistant infection than wealthy patients who seek medical care frequently.

Many experts agree that surveillance—keeping track—of antibiotic resistance in bacteria that cause human disease is a critical part of the picture. In 1992, less than $55,000 was spent on this type of antibiotic resistance surveillance by local, state, and federal governments combined.[1] Today, this effort is increasing. Surveillance for Emerging Antimicrobial Resistance Connected to Healthcare (SEARCH) is a network of hospitals, professional organizations, state health departments, and private companies that are voluntarily working together to report cases of *Staphylococcus aureus* which are resistant to vancomycin. By immediately reporting such cases to state health departments and the Centers for Disease Control and Prevention (CDC), this program assures that this dangerous pathogen is detected and reported. Surveillance programs such as this one are helping to monitor the problem of antibiotic resistance.

Infection Prevention

The simplest way to prevent outbreaks of drug-resistant disease is to do a better job of stopping infections from starting. One of the easiest ways to do this is for people to wash their hands frequently, especially before eating. Washing with plain old hot

Thorough hand washing is still the best way to prevent the spread of infection.

water and soap (antibacterial soaps are not necessary and may contribute to antibiotic resistance) can reduce the spread of disease. Of course, hand washing is particularly important for people in the medical field or those, such as teachers or child-care providers, who come into contact with many people during the day. Shaking hands, opening doors, using handrails, and speaking on telephones used by others are all ways to pick up harmful bacteria. Frequent hand washing can help prevent the organisms from entering the body. "Hands are the most dangerous thing in the hospital," says Dr. Robert A. Weinstein, director of infectious diseases for the Cook County Bureau of Health Services in Chicago.[2]

In some Asian countries, it is considered good manners for someone with a cold or flu to wear a mask to prevent the spread of germs. Yet in the United States, people go to work and school and attend public events when ill without much thought about the spread of their disease. Changing this practice could help reduce the chances of infecting others.

An even more effective way to prevent infections is through vaccination, the injection of a substance that prevents the person from getting a particular disease. Unfortunately, vaccines are not available for many diseases. In addition, people with the HIV virus have damaged immune systems, which can make vaccines less effective.

Educating Patients

Patients themselves are sometimes to blame for misuse of antibiotics. People have come to feel that a trip to the doctor should result in the doctor fixing the problem. Having experienced remarkable recoveries in the past due to antibiotics, they may demand antibiotics whether or not they are necessary. People also forget that their own immune system can cure most infections if given a chance. Doctors, not wanting unhappy patients, may write a prescription rather than spend time trying to explain to the patient that the antibiotic will do no good. Yet patients do need to be educated about proper antibiotic use.

As with many drugs, taking antibiotics incorrectly can cause more harm than not taking them at all. Patients may take too low a dose, perhaps reducing the amount to try to prevent side effects such as an upset stomach. Or they may miss doses. In these cases, not enough antibiotic gets to the bacteria. Some may be killed, but others (the stronger ones) may survive.

Pharmacists put stickers on prescription bottles of antibiotics, reminding patients to finish their prescriptions. This is because many patients stop taking their medicine as soon as they feel better. But stopping the medication before the prescribed period often results in some infected organisms surviving. The ones that survive are the ones best able to resist the antibiotic. These then continue to grow and breed.

Doctors and pharmacists also warn patients about saving antibiotics and using them later. Some people accumulate unfinished prescriptions and then use them when they suspect they or other family members have an infection. This self-treatment is also dangerous because the person may not have a bacterial infection. Even if bacteria are at fault, the particular antibiotic the person takes may not be one that works well for that particular type of bacteria. However, taking the antibiotic still kills off some bacteria (including helpful bacteria), while allowing others (the resistant ones) to thrive.

Encouraging "good" bacteria may also help reduce the need for antibiotics. In many cases, bacteria can protect people. Some ways to introduce protective bacteria include breastfeeding (the baby picks up bacteria from the mother's skin) and eating or drinking food products that contain lactobacillus, a common bacterium that causes no harm and can help rid the intestines of harmful bacteria.

Changing Prescribing Habits

A study reported in the English medical journal *Lancet* in 1996 found that up to 40 percent of people visiting their doctors for a cold were given antibiotics.[3] A similar study by the CDC showed that 42 percent of pediatricians surveyed in Georgia routinely prescribe antibiotics for patients with colds. In the past, many doctors have viewed the use of unnecessary antibiotics as a harmless way to satisfy the patient's demand for treatment. But increasingly, doctors are learning that this habit is harmful. "The better part of valor here," says Dr. Tina Tan, an infectious-disease specialist at Children's Memorial Hospital in Chicago, "is to err more on the conservative side and not prescribe an antibiotic for an upper respiratory tract infection."[4]

Another common practice among doctors is to rely on broad-spectrum antibiotics. Broad-spectrum antibiotics attack a wide range of bacteria rather than targeting the specific organism that is causing the problem. Doctors may prescribe these heavy hitters because they figure that, whatever bug is to blame, the drug will take care of it. Or they may use the broad-spectrum drug while waiting for the laboratory tests to identify the specific bacteria involved. Unfortunately, these broad-spectrum antibiotics not only kill off a lot of harmless or even helpful bacteria, they also promote the development of a wide range of drug-resistant organisms.

Ear infections are a common reason for doctors to prescribe antibiotics. As a result, about half of the bacteria that commonly cause ear infections are now believed to be resistant to antibiotics.[5] A study published in the April 2000 issue of the medical journal *Pediatrics* looked at a group of 383 patients of a pediatric practice in Rochester, New York, for one year. During this period, doctors carefully considered whether to use antibiotics for patients with colds or respiratory infections. They only gave antibiotics to children they believed (or lab tests showed) had bacterial infections. More than three-quarters of the patients in the study did not get antibiotics. The doctors found that withholding antibiotics in these cases did not result in more office visits or complications.[6] According to Dr. Michael Pichichero, one of the authors of the study, while some doctors prescribe antibiotics for nearly all patients who have colds or respiratory infections, "there is, however, no scientific rationale for such antibiotic use."[7]

Experts advise some additional steps for doctors to take to help prevent the spread of drug-resistant disease. Doctors may have to hold back on prescribing some antibiotics. They would use these antibiotics for only the most difficult cases. Studies have shown that when use of a particular antibiotic is restricted, resistance rates drop. Whenever possible, they should choose antibiotics after laboratory

The common cold is a virus, so antibiotics have no effect on it. Researchers continue to work toward a vaccine, however.

tests show which drugs will be most effective against the bacteria causing the problem. A simple, but often overlooked, precaution is that doctors should always wash their hands between patients.

Doctors may also have to spend more time with patients, talking to them about the proper use of antibiotics and following their progress. Howard Bauchner, M.D., professor of pediatrics at the Boston University School of Medicine, warns: " . . . if we do not start using antibiotics more judiciously now, we could lose our ability to fight infections."[8]

Another way doctors can help is to consider the patient's surroundings. For example, if all the patients in a hospital ward are being given the same antibiotic, chances are higher that resistant organisms will develop. On the other hand, if doctors prescribe a variety of different antibiotics, it would be more difficult for a drug-resistant organism to spread because chances are one of the antibiotics in use will kill it.

Doctors do not often think about it, but in a way, they change the balance of nature in an area whenever they introduce an antibiotic. Just as killing off all the foxes allows populations of geese to get so large that they become a problem in parks and on golf courses, killing off bacterial predators can allow other populations of bacteria to grow and become a problem. Whenever humans change the balance of nature, the consequences can be serious.

The CDC has come up with a way to encourage doctors to prescribe antibiotics responsibly. The CDC has developed a prescription pad, where instead of

Name: ———————————————— **Date:** ——/——/——
Diagnosis: ❑ Cold or Flu ❑ Middle ear fluid (Otitis Media with Effusion, OME)
❑ Cough   ❑ Viral sore throat
❑ Other: ——————————————————————

You have been diagnosed as having an illness caused by a virus.
Antibiotic treatment does not cure viral infections.
If given when not needed, antibiotics can be harmful. The
treatments prescribed below will help you feel better while your
body's own defenses are defeating the virus.

General instructions:
❑ Increase fluids.
❑ Use cool mist vaporizer or saline nasal spray to
relieve congestion.
❑ Soothe throat with ice chips, or sore
throat spray; lozenges for older children and adults.

Specific medicines:
❑ Fever or aches: ————————————————
❑ Congestion: ————————————————
❑ Cough: ————————————————
❑ Ear pain: ————————————————
❑ ————————————— : ——————————————
❑ ————————————— : ——————————————

Use medicines as directed by your doctor or the package
instructions. Stop the medication when the symptoms get better.

Follow up:
❑ If not improved in ____ days, if new symptoms occur,
or if you have other concerns, please call or return to the
office for a recheck.

❑ Other: ————————————————

CDC
CENTERS FOR DISEASE CONTROL
AND PREVENTION

Signed: ————————————————————————

*The CDC has prepared a prescription pad to help doctors
explain to patients that antibiotics do not cure infections that
are caused by viruses.*

writing a prescription for an antibiotic, doctors can write instructions for patients on how to take care of viral illnesses (drink plenty of fluids, rest, and so forth). The CDC has also produced brochures that explain to patients when antibiotics work and when they do not. The CDC hopes this will make doctors more comfortable with not prescribing antibiotics when patients ask for them. The American Academy of Pediatrics is also working to educate doctors and patients about the dangers of improper antibiotic use.

7

A Look Toward
the Future

*We worry about bioterrorism, but these little
bugs are bioterrorists every day.*

—U.S. Senator Barbara Mikulski

Just how resistant can drug-resistant
bacteria get? In 1990, a super-strain of
Staphylococcus could resist, to varying
degrees, thirty-one different drugs.[1] Some
strains of tuberculosis are resistant to two
or more of the drugs used to treat it, leading some to wonder whether the world will
see a return to the days before antibiotics
when a diagnosis of tuberculosis was a
death sentence.

New Super Bugs

Researchers fear that *Staphylococcus aureus* is developing resistance not just to methicillin, but also to the so-called drug of last resort, vancomycin. Already they have seen a few cases, including four in the United States, that are partially resistant to vancomycin. "It's a warning that fully resistant organisms may be on the horizon," says Julie Gerberding of the Centers for Disease Control and Prevention. "*Staph aureus* itself is a very invasive destructive organism," adds Michael Rybak, professor of pharmacy and medicine at Wayne State University in Detroit. "Add to that multidrug resistance . . . and it leaves very few options for physicians."[2]

In 1995, doctors found multi-drug-resistant *Yersinia pestis* in a specimen from a sixteen-year-old boy in Madagascar. This organism had been collected and tested between 1926 and 1995 without any sign of multi-drug resistance. Why would anyone be concerned? Well, because *Yersinia pestis* is the organism that causes plague. In the 1300s, the plague wiped out nearly a third of the population of Europe.

Could the world be in for a plague that could not be stopped with modern drugs? During the 1980s, the Soviet Union loaded incurable strains of bubonic plague into missile warheads aimed at the United States. They had created the strains through genetic engineering (changing the bacteria's genes). As this technology becomes more sophisticated, scientists may be able to mix genes of different organisms to create deadly biological weapons. According to Richard

A. Falkenrath, assistant professor of public policy at the John F. Kennedy School of Government at Harvard University, taking the same bacteria and viruses that cause disease naturally and using them as biological weapons could cause terrible diseases to spread unnaturally. This has the potential to cause catastrophic losses of life. "A biological weapon could use several different types of disease-causing germs," says Falkenrath, "including germs that have been made resistant to certain kinds of antimicrobial drugs." The possible use of resistant organisms is of great concern because it would make such an attack difficult to fight. As a result, the United States Department of Defense considers antibiotic resistance when they evaluate suspicious outbreaks of infectious disease that might have been caused by a biological weapon. "Fortunately," says Falkenrath, "advanced biological weapons have never been used in an attack against people—and we hope never will."[3]

Concern that a super bug might be the ultimate weapon of war has led the military to fund a variety of research projects. The Defense Department gave Isis Pharmaceuticals in Carlsbad, California, $6 million to look for a drug that could attack any bacteria—even ones scientists have not seen yet. The idea is to find a key substance that no bacteria can live without and then create a way to block it.[4] Scientists are not even sure such an element exists, but they are worried that a biological weapon made from genetically engineered bacteria could be hard to fight, particularly if it is purposely designed to be drug-resistant. Other researchers are working on vaccines for drug-resistant diseases. If any of these projects is successful, it could provide an answer to the peacetime problem of drug-resistant disease.

In 2000, the Clinton administration asked for an additional $65 million in the budget to develop a better way to watch for dangerous microorganisms. The proposed surveillance system included $40 million for possible biological weapons attacks, another $15 million for emerging infectious diseases (including antibiotic-resistant illnesses), and $10 million for food-borne illnesses.[5]

Emerging Viruses

It seemed like the end of the world. The disease started suddenly and spread like wildfire. It was not an ancient plague. It was influenza—flu. People called it "Spanish flu" even though it probably started in the United States, not Spain. But this flu was remarkably deadly. From 1918 to 1919, the flu epidemic swept around the world in less than five months. One out of every three people was sick. In some cities, ten thousand people a week died. In just six months, between 20 million and 40 million people around the world lost their lives. Ever since, scientists have wondered why it was so deadly.

Researchers are now examining the genetic structure of the virus, trying to understand how it operated. Might there have been a mutation in one of the virus's genes that made it turn deadly? Or did the virus somehow "learn" better ways of spreading and

A lab assistant analyzes a virus.

infecting new victims? Perhaps the people who died were less able to fight the virus for some reason. Unlike most modern flu victims, the people who died were healthy adults, aged twenty to forty, not the very young or the very old. Perhaps the most frightening question is: Why did the virus not kill everyone?[6]

Emerging viruses, viruses that are new or have not been seen before by researchers, are a prime area of concern to modern scientists. Researchers also keep an eye on viruses that pop up in new areas. The 1999 outbreak of West Nile virus in New York City, for example, took scientists by surprise. The virus had never before been seen in North America.

Experts estimated that the 1999 New York outbreak made sixty-two people sick and killed seven. As a result, scientists began to test for the virus early in 2000 in order to be prepared for new outbreaks. West Nile virus did reappear, and scientists continue to monitor its spread.

Monitoring emerging diseases is an ongoing effort. Scientists want to be prepared so that disasters like the 1918 epidemic do not happen again.

Change Existing Drugs

One tactic for fighting resistant organisms is to take a drug with a high resistance rate and blend it with a different drug that attacks the resistance mechanism in order to make a new drug. One example of this is Augmentin. It combines amoxicillin and clavulanic acid. Amoxicillin is an antibiotic that has been widely used for ear infections and other conditions. The number of prescriptions for amoxicillin went from 4.2 million a year in 1980 to an estimated 30 million in 1999.[7] As a result, bacteria have developed resistance to it. The addition of clavulanic acid, however, disarms the bacteria and lets the amoxicillin go in for the kill.

Another tactic researchers are using is to change existing antibiotics to make it more difficult for bacteria to break them down. Imipenem is a penicillin that has been changed in this way.

In April 1999, scientists at Princeton University announced that they had discovered a way to make vancomycin more powerful. This was an important discovery. Vancomycin has been the one antibiotic that doctors could count on when others failed. Recently, however, strains of bacteria have started to pop up that resist vancomycin to some degree. The scientists found that by making a few changes to the physical structure of the drug molecule, they made it work even more efficiently. It not only killed regular bacteria more quickly, but also killed off the strains that were resistant to vancomycin. By changing the way the drug acted, scientists were able to overcome the bacteria's ability to resist the drug. This sort of discovery may make it possible to make "old" drugs new again. It may also aid in the development of new

A scientist planning the evaluation of two experimental drugs.

antibiotics that can more effectively battle bacteria that are antibiotic-resistant.[8]

New Miracle Drugs

In Groton, Connecticut, there is an unusual zoo. There are no snack bars or polar bear exhibits. It is not even open to the public. In fact, only a few highly trained and well-protected "zookeepers" are allowed near it. It contains thousands of specimens, but they are all invisible . . . unless you view them through a microscope. This zoo is located at the Central Research facility of the Pfizer pharmaceutical company. It is where scientists in the company's Infectious Diseases department hold some of the most dangerous creatures on earth: bacteria that are resistant to most of the antibacterial weapons now known. These tough customers are being kept alive, not to entertain visitors or to preserve endangered species, but to use for testing new antibiotics.[9]

A new antibiotic takes nearly ten years and hundreds of millions of dollars to create.[10] However, profits from a successful drug can be extremely high, so companies continue to search for new and better antibiotics.

In 1999, a new antibiotic, Synercid, was approved to treat vancomycin-resistant *Enterococcus faecium* (VREF). This was an important tool in the war against VREF, which infects about fourteen thousand people a year.[11] Unfortunately, Synercid can only be given by injection, so patients have to stay in the hospital or be sent home with intravenous equipment

(equipment that gives the patients doses of medication through tubing into a vein).

On April 18, 2000, the Food and Drug Administration approved a new antibiotic, Zyvox. Zyvox was not just a new drug; it was from the first entirely new class of antibiotics.

Zyvox attacks bacteria at an earlier point in their development than other antibiotics. It blocks the formation of proteins that allow the bacteria to spread inside the body. Doctors hope that Zyvox will help in the battle against drug-resistant disease. Frederick J. Angulo of the Centers for Disease Control and Prevention said: "This looks like a very positive addition. If this new class of drugs does work against the multi-drug-resistant [bacteria] we are seeing, then it will be a very useful treatment."[12]

When Syncercid was released in 1999, it was approved to treat multi-drug-resistant bacteria. Both Synercid and Zyvox have been found effective against *Enterococcus faecium* bacteria. This organism is common in hospitals and has become increasingly resistant to other antibiotics, including vancomycin. However, scientists warn that bacteria may develop resistance to Synercid more quickly, due to its similarity to Virginiamycin, an antibiotic commonly used to feed animals that are then eaten by humans. There are no animal antibiotics similar to Zyvox, however. Even so, Zyvox is not a solution to the problem of drug-resistant infections. It only works against certain bacteria, and in studies on patients with the toughest infections, Zyvox was only able to cure two out of three patients. Plus, in what could be the first

Researchers inspect the results of a test involving an antibacterial drug.

sign of danger, during the testing that took place before Zyvox was approved for the public, a few patients with VREF had infections that were also resistant to Zyvox. For this reason, government officials warned doctors to use Zyvox only when absolutely necessary. "It is likely that in time that resistance will develop," said Dr. David M. Bell, an expert in antibiotic resistance at the Beth Israel Medical Center in Boston. "So we need to use these new drugs judiciously."[13]

The race for new antibiotics is a difficult one. "The reality," says Alan Proctor, executive director of Discovery Research, a part of Pfizer, Inc., "is that bacteria are powerfully inventive and, with time, become resistant to whatever we throw at them. But each time we come up with a new product, we buy patients a valuable window of time."[14]

Researchers are searching everywhere for new weapons in the fight against bacteria. Some of the places they are looking may seem surprising. For example, scientists are studying the ways in which other animals defend themselves against infection. Some have "host defense peptides," substances that can punch holes in bacterial cell walls. Researchers have also found antibiotic-like substances on the skin of frogs. Some of the compounds already under development have come from such unusual sources as moths, beetles, sharks, and cow saliva. Scientists are even looking for new sources among bacteria recovered from miles beneath the earth's surface.

Scientists are also studying plants. Dr. Kim Lewis, a biotechnology professor at Tufts University working with Dr. Frank Stermitz, a chemist at Colorado State University, recently discovered a plant that may be able to help with the fight against drug-resistant *Staphylococcus aureus*. Their quest took them not into the Amazon rainforest, but into their own backyards. The plant, barberry, is a common shrub. However, barberry produces a natural antibiotic called berberin. It is not very effective as an antibiotic because bacteria easily pump it out of their cells. However, the scientists reasoned that there must be some reason for the barberry bush to keep making berberin. What they found is that the barberry also makes a substance that inhibits the

Scientists are even studying plants to look for answers in the fight against drug-resistant bacteria.

bacteria's pump, allowing the berberin to do its job. One substance disables the pump, while the other kills the bacterium. "When you take these compounds and combine them," says Lewis, "it kills *staph*. We're borrowing an approach that the plant has been using and [we're] using it for our own purposes."[15] Lewis is now expanding his work to examine other plants. He hopes that some of these antibiotic/pump inhibitor combinations will lead to drugs that are effective against antibiotic-resistant bacteria.

Other clues to new antibiotics may come from the bacteria themselves. Just as Selman Waksman worked with the bacteria in soil in 1943 to develop streptomycin, today's scientists are examining bacteria to see how they defend themselves against other bacteria. In fact, one of the newest antibiotics, Synercid, was developed from an organism found in a soil sample from Argentina, a country in South America.

It may also be possible to harness the natural enemies of bacteria, tiny viruses called bacteriophages. Bacteriophages are so small that a single drop of tap water may contain one billion of them. Bacteriophages, or "phages," not only attack bacteria, they target one bacterial species and therefore do not harm the host. The phage attaches itself to the wall of the bacteria cell and gradually injects itself inside. There it takes over the cell's genetic machinery, turning it into a factory production line that punches out copies of the phage. Eventually, the bacterium actually explodes.

In areas of the former Soviet Union, hospitals

have used phages to treat infections for many years. While American researchers abandoned bacteriophages when penicillin came on the scene, Soviet researchers continued to perfect phage treatment. Now that antibiotic resistance has reached the crisis stage, American scientists are once again taking a look at these powerful little weapons. "I'm convinced that bacteriophages will work," said Carl Merril, chief of the biochemical genetics laboratory at the National Institutes of Health. He admits, however, that people may not readily accept a new treatment coming from the former Soviet Union. "It's unusual, to say the least," he said. People view the region as falling apart, financially ruined, and in desperate need of modern advances. Yet phage treatment may become a promising option. "We've been using phages for years," said a doctor from Tbilisi, in the Republic of Georgia, while the hospital lights flickered. "There are no major side effects. They're a living, natural force, not a toxic chemical. I wish our electricity were as reliable!"[16] The researchers have even had success with a kind of bandage soaked with a solution of different phages to treat infected burns.

It may also be possible for scientists to develop drugs that disarm bacteria, leaving them alive but less able to cause harm. These "anti-virulence" drugs might add another weapon to the doctor's bag.

Scientists are learning more about how bacteria operate. For example, some form biofilms, slimy walls of bacteria that keep out antibiotics, detergents, and the body's own immune system weapons. Certain types of bacteria can sense how many of their species are present. They may also use this sensing to tell when they have reached the right location in the human body. Some researchers suspect that bacteria may even be able to send signals that trick the human host into not responding properly to the infection. "Different species of bacteria have different capabilities, but they work together," explains Bonnie Bassler, a microbial geneticist at Princeton University. "They're behaving like multicellular organisms. That's really smart."[17] By learning how bacteria sense or communicate, scientists may be able to disrupt their signals or trick them into sending the wrong signals. Some scientists are also working on using bacterial signals to make bacteria produce natural antibiotics.

With tuberculosis, scientists are working on the genetic code of *Mycobacterium tuberculosis*, the organism that causes the disease. They are hoping to find clues about how the disease works. It may be that a new type of drug could attack the organism while it is hiding in its dormant state.

Scientists are also working on the genetic code of the malaria parasite. In November 1999, scientists at the National Institute of Allergy and Infectious Diseases produced the first detailed genetic map of *Plasmodium falciparum*, the deadliest of the malaria parasites. The map will help scientists locate genes important to drug resistance and disease severity.[18] Knowing how the organism's genes work may also help scientists develop more effective drugs.

In 2000, scientists in Australia discovered how the malaria parasite resists treatment. They found that a protein called Pgh1 is involved in changing a gene to keep the drug from building up in the parasite's cells. The altered gene either stops the antimalaria drugs from entering the cell or rapidly pumps them out. This knowledge may help scientists develop a way to reverse the process, which would make existing drugs effective again.[19]

One novel idea is to use the body's own bacteria as a weapon. Gregor Reid, of The Lawson Research Institute in Canada and a professor of microbiology and immunology at the University of Western Ontario, explains: "This approach of using bacteria to promote health is called 'probiotics'—'pro' for promoting health, rather than 'anti' in antibiotics." Dr. Reid says that hundreds of millions of people in Europe and Japan already eat probiotic products (foods and drinks that contain "good" bacteria). "We have discovered certain types of lactobacilli [bacteria commonly used to make cheese and yogurt] which help restore and maintain health in the intestine, urinary and genital tracts. We hope one day soon to give them to people so that they can remain healthy, as well as better fight off infections." These substances could also be made in the form of a capsule to swallow. "Remember, we eat bacteria every day whether we like it or not," says Dr. Reid. "It's our 'good' bacteria which help us digest our food and break down nasty toxins in our gut. So, by keeping up the number of good bugs, we could prevent bad ones, including those that resist antibiotics, from causing harm. In limited situations, we may even be able to treat infections with good bugs." The good bacteria could even be frozen and stored for future use. Dr. Reid cautions that some of the products now being sold as probiotics have not been proven scientifically. However, he predicts that probiotics and similar health-oriented foods will one day have a huge impact.[20]

Vaccines may offer the greatest hope. In the case of tuberculosis, for example, all 2 billion of the people already infected could be vaccinated to prevent the disease from ever becoming active. Such a vaccine would be a challenge, however. Scientists predict it may take twenty years to develop.[21]

Scientists have had difficulty developing a vaccine for malaria because the parasite that causes it gets inside red blood cells, where the immune system (including antibodies created by a vaccination) cannot see it. It has many stages, during which it changes its identity, making it even harder to attack. Parasites of the same species but from other geographic locations can be different enough that a vaccine that protects against one may not work against another. The structure of the malaria parasite is also complex. It has a thousand times as many genes as the HIV virus that causes AIDS.

Most malaria vaccine research efforts have concentrated on the *Plasmodium falciparum* parasite because it causes the most severe form of the disease. Some experimental vaccines target specific stages of development of the malaria parasite, but these each have limitations. One possible solution would be a vaccine "cocktail" that combined several of these kinds of vaccines. Scientists, however, do not know if a cocktail would work. In any case, such testing is still in the future. For now, malaria is still a threat, and one that may well get worse while no solution is found.

Beating the Superbugs—Solving the Problem of Drug-resistant Disease

Humans, like other animals, begin life without bacteria and without antibiotic resistance. From the moment of birth, they become home to some of the millions of bacteria in their environment. The bacteria they take on are the ones most common in their immediate surroundings . . . until they start taking antibiotics. Then they become part of a process that selects stronger, more resistant bacteria. And that is where the problem of drug-resistant disease begins.

The war on drug-resistant disease will be fought on several fronts. Scientists say that one goal for the future is to make an effort to keep the level of resistant bacteria in a person's body low from the beginning. This would limit the ability of disease-causing bacteria to take on resistance from harmless bacteria and would help doctors control infection in people. New, more effective drugs will also play a large role in the battle against the super bugs. Watching for emerging diseases, improving infection-control measures, and eliminating misuse of antibiotics is also part of the battle.

Scientists disagree about how dangerous the drug resistance trend really is. But they agree that as drug resistance grows, the danger increases. "You're dealing with living microbes that have shown an incredible ability to accommodate antibiotics and come out winning," says Linda Tollefson, director of surveillance and compliance in the Food and Drug Administration's Center for Veterinary Medicine. "We have no idea what they are going to do next. Our fear is that we're seeing the tip of the iceberg."[22]

Chronology

1674—Anton van Leeuwenhoek discovers "wee animalcules" (bacteria) using a homemade microscope.

1864—The "germ theory of disease" and Louis Pasteur's idea that microbes are present in the air and settle onto exposed living tissue are officially endorsed by the French Academy of Sciences.

1881—Robert Koch introduces a way to grow and distinguish bacteria. He uses a mixture of potato extract, gelatin, and agar. A single bacterium placed on this mixture can multiply into a colony of hundreds of millions overnight.

1888—E. de Freudenreich finds that a solution made by the blue-pus bacterium (*Bacillus pyocyaneus*, now known as *Pseudomonas aeruginosa*) stops the growth of other bacteria. The substance, named pyocyanase, is the first natural antibiotic product (one not made by chemists) to be discovered. Its activity suggests that bacteria produce substances that might be useful for treating human disease.

1905—German scientist Paul Ehrlich develops the concept of "magic bullets," drugs that would target certain types of bacteria and kill them, leaving the human host unharmed.

1910—Salvarsan, the first effective antibacterial compound, comes on the market. Developed by Paul Ehrlich, Salvarsan sparks new interest in developing antibacterial drugs.

1928—Scottish scientist Alexander Fleming discovers penicillin.

1937—An Englishman describes the first case of drug-resistant disease after noticing several patients have failed to improve after taking sulfonamide.

1939—Howard Florey and Ernst Chain set up a system for growing penicillin mold in quantities large enough to treat a human patient.

1941—Selman Waksman suggests the term "antibiotic" to describe antibacterial agents.

1942—The Cocoanut Grove fire provides a test for penicillin and prompts the government to back pharmaceutical companies to produce it in large quantities.

1957—John C. Sheehan completes work on synthesized penicillin, creating a practical way to produce penicillin in large quantities.

1950s—*Staphylococcus*, a common skin bacterium, becomes resistant to penicillin.

1960s—Strains of *Staphylococcus* first show signs of resistance to methicillin, leaving only vancomycin, "the drug of last resort," as an effective weapon.

1970—The National Nosocomial Infections Surveillance System is established to gather information on hospital-acquired infections.

1987—Vancomycin-resistant *enterococci* are first reported in England and France.

1997—A strain of *Staphylococcus aureus* that is resistant to all known antibiotics (including vancomycin) shows up in Japan.

2000—Zyvox, one of a new class of antibiotics, is approved by the Food and Drug Administration. It is the first new family of antibiotics to be introduced in decades.

Appendix

What You Can Do to Help Stop the Spread of Drug-resistant Diseases

1. Reduce the spread of bacteria by thoroughly washing your hands for at least twenty seconds with very warm water and soap, especially before and after eating or handling food. Washing hands is the single most important thing you can do to prevent an infection.

2. If you have a contagious infection, avoid contact with others.

3. Minimize your use of antibacterial products such as soaps, cleaners, and household products. These products may actually do more harm than good. Hot water and detergents or soaps are effective germ killers and do not promote resistant bacteria.

4. Keep your vaccinations up to date. It is easier to prevent a serious disease than to treat it.

5. If you are otherwise healthy and have a cold or respiratory infection, do not ask for an antibiotic unless the doctor has performed tests that indicate a bacterial infection or strongly suspects you have one.

6. If your doctor suggests an antibiotic, ask why you need one. Find out how and when to take it and for how long. Ask whether there are any foods, drinks, or activities you should avoid while taking the medication. Let the doctor know if you are taking any other medicines.

7. When taking an antibiotic, follow the instructions carefully. Do not stop taking the medication early unless the doctor tells you to. Do not skip doses, take less than directed, borrow or share antibiotics, or save unused medicine for future use.

8. Avoid items likely to contain disease-causing organisms, such as rare hamburgers, under-cooked eggs or chicken, raw fish or shellfish, and unwashed fruits or vegetables.

9. Always store foods at the proper temperature. Do not eat cooked foods left at room temperature for more than two hours.

10. Never taste cake or cookie batter containing raw eggs.

11. Never use utensils, plates, cutting boards, or containers that have touched raw meat for cooked foods.

12. Throw out foods that are beyond the "use by" date. "When in doubt, throw it out."

13. Never drink water from streams, springs, or other sources that have not been verified as safe.

14. Exercise, eat healthy foods, and get plenty of sleep. These activities boost your immune system, which helps you fight off infections.

Chapter Notes

Chapter 1. Antibiotic Resistance

1. Amanda Spake, "Losing the Battle of the Bugs," *U.S. News & World Report*, May 10, 1999, p. 52.

2. Ibid., p. 55.

3. Ibid., p. 60.

4. Stuart B. Levy, *The Antibiotic Paradox: How Miracle Drugs Are Destroying the Miracle* (New York: Plenum Press, 1992), p. 129.

5. Sheryl Gay Stolberg, "After 4 Deaths, Scientists Fear Germ's Threat," *The New York Times*, August 20, 1999, p. A17.

6. Associated Press, "4 Die of Drug-Resistant Staph," *Newsday,* August 20, 1999, p. A72.

7. Sheryl Gay Stolberg, "F.D.A. Approves New Drug to Attack Resistant Germs," *The New York Times*, April 19, 2000, p. A19.

8. Ricki Lewis, "The Rise of Antibiotic-Resistant Infections," *FDA Consumer,* vol. 29, no. 7, September 1995, p. 12.

9. Laurie Garrett, *The Coming Plague: Newly Emerging Diseases in a World Out of Balance* (New York: Farrar, Straus and Giroux, 1994), p. 431.

10. Spake, pp. 55–56.

11. Jeffrey Goldberg, "Microbes on the Move," *New York Times Magazine*, October 10, 1999, p. 21.

12. Michael Balter, "AIDS Now World's Fourth Biggest Killer," *Science*, vol. 284, no. 5417, May 14, 1999, p. 1101.

13. WHO, "Medicines Are Losing Their Effectiveness," *Removing Obstacles to Healthy Development: World Health Organization Report on Infectious Diseases*, World Health Organization, Geneva, 1999, <http://www.who.org/infectious-disease-report/pages/ch12text.html,1999> (February 12, 2000).

14. Nicholas Wade, "Decoding a Radiation-Resistant Bug," *The New York Times,* November 19, 1999, A30.

Chapter 2. Super Bugs: Killer Bacteria and Viruses

1. Stuart B. Levy, *The Antibiotic Paradox: How Miracle Drugs Are Destroying the Miracle* (New York: Plenum Press, 1992), p. 147.

2. Elizabeth Olson, "Antibiotic Misuse Turns Treatable to Incurable," *The New York Times*, June 13, 2000, p. F2.

3. Tamar Nordenberg, "Miracle Drugs vs. Superbugs," *FDA Consumer*, vol. 32, no. 6, November–December, 1998, p. 23.

4. *Antimicrobial Resistance: A Growing Threat to Public Health*, Centers for Disease Control and Prevention, June 1999.

5. M.A.J. McKenna, "Hospital Infections Raise Growing Alarm, Here and Worldwide," *The Atlanta Journal and Constitution*, March 7, 2000, p. C1.

6. *Antimicrobial Resistance: A Growing Threat to Public Health*.

7. McKenna, p. C1.

8. Associated Press, "4 Die of Drug-Resistant Staph," *Newsday*, August 20, 1999, p. A72.

9. Anita Manning, "A Bug the Drugs Can't Get Rid Of," *USA Today*, March 9, 2000, p. 9D.

10. Laurie Garrett, "TB Deaths Soaring Worldwide: Drug-Resistance Growth is Cited," *Newsday*, March 24, 2000, p. A32.

11. Leslie Roberts, "The Comeback Plague," *U.S. News & World Report*, March 27, 2000, p. 50.

12. *Tuberculosis*, World Health Organization, Geneva, 1999.

13. Judy Mann, "In the Long Run, It's Not Cheap to Ignore TB," *The Washington Post*, March 22, 2000, p. C15.

14. *Tuberculosis*, World Health Organization, Geneva, April 2000.

15. Susan Aldridge, *Magic Molecules: How Drugs Work* (Cambridge, U.K.: Cambridge University Press, 1998), p. 60.

16. David Brown, "TB Resistance Stands at 11% of Cases," *The Washington Post*, March 24, 2000, p. A14.
17. Garrett, p. A32.
18. Donald G. McNeil, Jr., "Resisting Drugs, TB Spreads Fast in the West," *The New York Times*, March 24, 2000, p. A10.

Chapter 3. Magic Bullets: Antibiotics as Miracle Drugs

1. Stuart B. Levy, *The Antibiotic Paradox: How Miracle Drugs Are Destroying the Miracle* (New York: Plenum Press, 1992), p. 19.
2. Ibid., p. 22.
3. "Counterattack on Germs," *Pfizer, Inc.*, <http://www.pfizer.com/science/counterattack.html> (February 5, 2000).
4. Levy, p. 33.
5. John C. Sheehan, *The Enchanted Ring: The Untold Story of Penicillin* (Cambridge, Mass.: The MIT Press, 1983), p. 37.
6. Susan Aldridge, *Magic Molecules: How Drugs Work* (Cambridge, U.K.: Cambridge University Press, 1998), p. 70.
7. Sheehan, p. 1.
8. Levy, pp. 1–5.
9. Ibid., p. 7.
10. Aldridge, p. 72.
11. *Antibiotic Resistance: A New Threat to Your and Your Family's Health*, Centers for Disease Control and Prevention, April 12, 1999.
12. M.A.J. McKenna, "Superbugs' Resisting a Leading Antibiotic," *The Atlanta Journal and Constitution*, January 7, 2000, p. A1.

Chapter 4. Antibiotics: Too Much of a Good Thing?

1. *Antibiotic Resistance: A New Threat to Your and Your Family's Health*, Centers for Disease Control and Prevention, April 12, 1999.
2. Amanda Spake, "Losing the Battle of the Bugs," *U.S. News & World Report*, May 10, 1999, p. 52.

3. Ricki Lewis, "The Rise of Antibiotic-Resistant Infections," *FDA Consumer*, vol. 29, no. 7, September 1995, p. 13.

4. Stuart B. Levy, *The Antibiotic Paradox: How Miracle Drugs Are Destroying the Miracle* (New York: Plenum Press, 1992), p. 127.

5. *Antimicrobial Resistance—Data to Assess Public Health Threat From Resistant Bacteria Are Limited*, United States General Accounting Office, Washington, D.C., April 28, 1999, p. 16.

6. Lawrence Osborne, "A Stalinist Antibiotic Alternative," *The New York Times Magazine*, February 6, 2000, p. 54.

7. Karen Goldberg Goff, "Antibacterial Agents Can Create Own Problems," *The Washington Times*, September 26, 1999, p. D3.

8. *Antimicrobial Resistance—Data to Assess Public Health Threat From Resistant Bacteria Are Limited*, United States General Accounting Office, Washington, D.C., April 28, 1999, p. 4.

9. "Antibiotics: 'Miracle Drugs' are Losing Ground to Infections," *The Mayo Clinic Health Oasis*, September 1997, <http://www.mayohealth.org/mayo/9710/htm/antibiot.htm> (April 7, 2000).

10. *Antibiotic Resistance: A New Threat to Your and Your Family's Health*, Centers for Disease Control and Prevention, April 12, 1999.

11. Elizabeth Neus, "Health Departments Cannot Track Drug-Resistant Disease, Report Says," Gannett News Service, February 26, 1999, p. ARC.

12. Spake, p. 60.

13. John Carey, "Outsmarting the Virus," *Business Week*, February 22, 1999, p. 142.

14. Laurie Garrett, "New Deadlier HIV? Multidrug-Resistant Strains Worry 3 Research Teams," *Newsday*, September 22, 1999, p. A3.

15. Carey, p. 143.

16. Levy, pp. 113–114.

17. "Medicines Are Losing Their Effectiveness," *Removing Obstacles to Healthy Development: World Health Organization Report on Infectious Diseases*, World Health

Organization, Geneva, 1999, <http://www.who.org/ infectious-disease-report/pages/ch12text.html, 1999> (February 12, 2000).

18. Levy, p. 239.

19. *Antimicrobial Resistance: A Growing Threat to Public Health*, Centers for Disease Control and Prevention, June 1999.

20. Hospital Infections Program Brochure, Centers for Disease Control and Prevention, June 26, 1999.

21. Laurie Garrett, "TB Deaths Soaring Worldwide: Drug-Resistance Growth is Cited," *Newsday*, March 24, 2000, p. A32.

22. Donald G. McNeil, Jr., "Resisting Drugs, TB Spreads Fast in the West," *The New York Times*, March 24, 2000, p. A10.

Chapter 5. Antibiotics and Food

1. Marc Kaufman, "Worries Rise Over Effect of Antibiotics in Animal Feed," *The Washington Post*, March 17, 2000, p. A1.

2. Edwin W. Brown, "The Deadly War That We're Losing," *Medical Update*, vol. 22, December 1, 1998, p. 1.

3. Anita Manning, "Like a Resistant Strain, the Debate Won't Go Away," *USA Today*, June 15, 1999, p. 6D.

4. *Antibiotic Resistance: A New Threat to Your and Your Family's Health*, Centers for Disease Control and Prevention, April 12, 1999.

5. Manning, p. 6D.

6. Susan Aldridge, *Magic Molecules: How Drugs Work* (Cambridge, U.K.: Cambridge University Press, 1998), p. 80.

7. Kaufman, pp. A1.

8. Denise Grady, "Bacteria Cases in Denmark Cause Antibiotics Concerns in U.S.," *The New York Times*, November 4, 1999, p. A15.

9. Nicole St. Pierre, "Using Chicken Feed in the War on Superbugs," *Business Week*, February 14, 2000, p. 82.

10. Kaufman, p. A15.

11. "Food Safety: The Agricultural Use of Antibiotics and Its Implications for Human Health," United States General Accounting Office, Washington, D.C., April 28, 1999, pp. 4, 23–24.

12. Nicols Fox, *It Was Probably Something You Ate* (New York: Penguin Books, 1999), p. 26.

13. Kaufman, p. A15.

14. "Food Safety: The Agricultural Use of Antibiotics and Its Implications for Human Health," United States General Accounting Office, Washington, D.C., April 28, 1999, p. 24.

15. Laurie Garrett, *The Coming Plague: Newly Emerging Diseases in a World Out of Balance* (New York: Farrar, Straus and Giroux, 1994), p. 421.

16. Ibid, pp. 428–429.

17. Fox, pp. 103–105.

18. Garrett, p. 430.

19. Stuart B. Levy, *The Antibiotic Paradox: How Miracle Drugs Are Destroying the Miracle* (New York: Plenum Press, 1992), p. 137.

20. Ibid., pp.145–147.

21. Stuart B. Levy, "The Challenge of Antibiotic Resistance," *Scientific American*, March 1998, p. 51.

Chapter 6. Doctors Fight Back

1. David P. Fidler, "Legal Issues Associated with Antimicrobial Drug Resistance," *Emerging Infectious Diseases*, vol. 4, no. 2, April-June 1998, <http://www.cdc.gov/ncidod/eid/vol4no2/fidler.htm> (February 26, 2000).

2. Emily Yoffe, "Doctors Are Reminded, 'Wash Up!'" *The New York Times*, November 9, 1999, p. F1.

3. Susan Aldridge, *Magic Molecules: How Drugs Work* (Cambridge, U.K.: Cambridge University Press, 1998), p. 79.

4. Lindsey Tanner, "Use of Antibiotics for Kids Studied," *AP Online*, April 3, 2000.

5. Judy Foreman, "Flu Season Raises Antibiotics Dilemma: Opportunities for Needless Use Abound, Say Doctors, CDC," *Minneapolis Star Tribune*, February 7, 1999, p. 5E.

6. "Caution on Antibiotics," *Newsday*, April 2000, p. A22.

7. Tanner.

8. Tinker Ready and Elizabeth Shaw, "Antibiotics Overkill: The Number of Drug-Proof Bacteria Is Growing—Rapidly. Here's What You Need to Know to Keep Baby Safe," *Baby Talk*, February 1, 2000, pp. 38+.

Chapter 7. A Look Toward the Future

1. Laurie Garrett, *The Coming Plague: Newly Emerging Diseases in a World Out of Balance* (New York: Farrar, Straus and Giroux, 1994) p. 413.

2. Anita Manning, "A Bug the Drugs Can't Get Rid Of," *USA Today*, March 9, 2000, p. 9D.

3. Personal interview via e-mail with Richard A. Falkenrath, April 28, 2000.

4. Evelyn L. Wright, "Taking Aim at the Nightmare Bug," *Business Week*, November 1, 1999, p. 78.

5. Elizabeth Neus, "Health Departments Cannot Track Drug-Resistant Disease, Report Says," Gannett News Service, February 26, 1999, p. ARC.

6. Ruth Larson, "Fatal Flu Virus Lurked Many Years; Emerged to Cause 1918 Pandemic, Leaving Millions Dead," *The Washington Times*, February 16, 1999, p. A1.

7. Tinker Ready and Elizabeth Shaw, "Antibiotics Overkill: The Number of Drug-Proof Bacteria Is Growing—Rapidly. Here's What You Need to Know to Keep Baby Safe," *Baby Talk*, February 1, 2000, pp. 38+.

8. Reuters, "Antibiotic Wars: Scientists May Outwit Resistant Bacteria," 1999, ABC News.com, April 16, 1999, <http://www.abcnews.go.com/sections/living/DailyNews/antibiotics990416.html> (February 12, 2000).

9. "Counterattack on Germs," *Pfizer, Inc.*, 2000, <http://www.pfizer.com/science/counterattack.html> (February 5, 2000).

10. Mayo Clinic, "Antibiotics: 'Miracle Drugs' Are Losing Ground to Infections," The Mayo Clinic Health Oasis, September 1997, <http://www.mayohealth.org/mayo/9710/htm/antibiot.htm> (April 7, 2000).

11. Sheryl Gay Stolberg, "F.D.A. Approves New Drug to Attack Resistant Germs," *The New York Times*, April 19, 2000, p. A19.

12. Marc Kaufman, "FDA Panel Clears New Antibiotic," *The Washington Post*, March 25, 2000, p. A3.

13. Stolberg, p. A19.

14. "Counterattack on Germs," Pfizer, Inc., 2000, <http://www.pfizer.com/science/counterattack.html> (February 5, 2000).

15. Mary Anne Anderson, "Tufts Prof Fights 'Supergerm,'" University Wire, March 10, 2000.

16. Lawrence Osborne, "A Stalinist Antibiotic Alternative," *The New York Times Magazine*, February 6, 2000, pp. 50–51.

17. Evelyn Strauss, "A Symphony of Bacterial Voices," *Science*, vol. 284, no. 5418, May 12, 1999, p. 1304.

18. *NIH Scientists Create First Detailed Genetic Map of Malaria Parasite*, National Institute of Allergy and Infectious Diseases, November 11, 1999.

19. Fed: Scientists Pin Down Malaria Resistance Protein," AAP General News (Australia), February 24, 2000; Rich Callahan, "Malaria's Drug Resistance Studied," *AP Online*, February 23, 2000.

20. Personal interview via e-mail with Gregor Reid, April 7, 2000.

21. Leslie Roberts, "The Comeback Plague," *U.S. News & World Report,* March 27, 2000, p. 51.

22. Tamar Nordenberg, "Miracle Drugs vs. Superbugs," *FDA Consumer*, vol. 32, no. 6, November–December, 1998, p. 23.

Glossary

antibiotics—Natural substances made by living organisms such as molds or bacteria that kill or inhibit the growth of other microorganisms. (This term is now used also to refer to synthetic, or manufactured, versions of these natural substances.)

antimicrobials—Substances that kill, inhibit the growth, or prevent the harmful action of microbes.

bacteria—Microscopic, one-celled living organisms found on surfaces and on and in animal's (including human's) bodies.

bactericidal—A type of antibiotic that kills bacteria.

bacteriophage—Viruses that attack bacteria.

bacteriostatic—A type of antibiotic that inhibits the growth of bacteria.

broad-spectrum antibiotics—Drugs that kill a wide variety of bacteria.

host—The animal (human or other) that is home to the bacteria.

microbes—Microscopic organisms, including bacteria and viruses.

microorganism—An organism (plant or animal) that cannot be seen unless one uses a microscope.

MRSA—Methicillin-resistant *Staphylococcus aureus*, a potentially dangerous organism that is becoming a frequent cause of hospital-acquired infections.

narrow-spectrum antibiotics—Drugs that target a few specific types of bacteria.

nosocomial infections—Bacterial infections that are acquired ("caught") while in the hospital.

parasite—An organism that lives on or in another organism and gets food from it.

pathogen—Disease-causing organism.

pathogenic bacteria—Bacteria that are harmful to plants or animals (including humans).

plasmids—Small, circular pieces of DNA that contain additional genetic information. Plasmids carry genes that provide bacteria with survival skills, including instructions on how to resist antibiotics.

resistant—Able to avoid being affected by something. When bacteria are exposed to an antibiotic, some may be killed while others (those that are resistant) survive.

selective pressure—The process by which antibiotics actually encourage resistance by "selecting" bacteria able to survive (they kill all others).

sporulation—A process by which bacteria toughen their cell walls and become dormant as a means of protection in the face of antibiotics or other threats. They are able to later emerge and become active after the threat has passed.

super bugs—Bacteria that are resistant to many different antibiotics.

susceptible—Vulnerable; likely to be affected by. When bacteria are exposed to an antibiotic and the antibiotic kills them, the bacteria are said to be susceptible to that antibiotic.

vaccine—A drug that provides long-term immunity against a disease.

virus—A type of microbe that is significantly smaller than bacteria and that cannot grow or reproduce except within living cells. Most biologists consider viruses infectious particles, not living things. Antibiotics attack bacteria but do not harm viruses.

Further Reading

Altman, Linda Jacobs. *Plague and Pestilence: A History of Infectious Disease*. Berkeley Heights, N.J.: Enslow Publishers, 1998.

Desalle, Rob, ed. *Epidemic! The World of Infectious Diseases*. New York: New Press, 1999.

Farrell, Jeanette. *Invisible Enemies: Stories of Infectious Disease*. New York: Farrar, Straus & Giroux, 1998.

Friedlander, Mark P. and Leonard T. Kurland. *Outbreak: Disease Detectives at Work*. Minneapolis, Minn.: Lerner Publications, 2000.

Latta, Sara L. *Food Poisoning and Foodborne Diseases*. Berkeley Heights, N.J.: Enslow Publishers, 1999.

Internet Addresses

American Medical Association
Reports on Antibiotic Resistance
<http://www.ama-assn.org/ama/pub/article/
    1863-3643.html>

The Centers for Disease Control and Prevention (CDC)
Division of Bacterial and Mycotic Diseases: Antibiotic
    Resistance
<http://www.cdc.gov/antibioticresistance>

Microbe Zoo
<http://commtechlab.msu.edu/sites/dlc-me/zoo>

Stalking the Mysterious Microbe
<http://www.microbe.org>

The Why Files—Microbes: What Doesn't Kill Them
    Makes Them Stronger
<http://whyfiles.org/038badbugs>

World Health Organization
Communicable Disease Surveillance and Response
<http://www.who.int/emc>

Organizations

The Alliance for the Prudent Use of Antibiotics (APUA)
75 Kneeland Street
Boston, MA 02111–1901
(617) 636-0966
<http://www.healthsci.tufts.edu/apua>

The American Academy of Pediatrics
141 Northwest Point Boulevard
Elk Grove Village, IL 60007–1098
(847) 434-4000
<http://www.aap.org>

The Centers for Disease Control and Prevention (CDC)
1600 Clinton Road
Atlanta, GA 30333
(404) 639-3311
<http://www.cdc.gov>

World Health Organization
Avenue Appia 20
1211 Geneva 27
Switzerland
e-mail:info@who.int
<http://www.who.int>

Index